£1·20

Haunted Royal Homes

Haunted
Royal Homes

JOAN FORMAN

HARRAP

London

For
Thelma and Richard,
with love

First published in Great Britain 1987
by HARRAP Ltd
19-23 Ludgate Hill, London EC4M 7PD

ISBN 0–245–54516–6

Designed by Kirby-Sessions, London
Phototypeset by Falcon Graphic Art Ltd
Wallington, Surrey
Printed and bound by R.J. Acford
Chichester, Sussex

CONTENTS

ACKNOWLEDGMENTS

I gratefully acknowledge help received from the many owners, custodians, administrators and staff of the properties referred to in this book, and convey warm thanks for their unfailing patience and friendly cooperation in answering questions and giving information.

In particular I should like to mention the following:

HRH Princess Alice, Duchess of Gloucester, Lady Ashcombe, David Baldwin, The Duke and Duchess of Buccleuch, Joy Cope, David Duff, Vivien and Donald Ferrier, Lavender and Pat Gilmore, Jean Goodman, Mary Grainger, Tony Hutcheson, Steve Ingram, the late Tom Litchfield, Colonel T.D. Lloyd-Jones, Major-General and Mrs MacLellan, Bill McMinn, Doreen McPherson, Denis Mead, Peggy Mitchell, Eleanor O'Keeffe (Society of Psychical Research), Major Claud Rebbeck, The Scottish Tourist Board, the Earl and Countess of Strathmore, Mr W. Stewart, Nicholas Warliker, Colonel D.J.C. Wickes and Walter 'Wally' Wyles.

Additional appreciation is due to Pauline Merchant for typing with exemplary speed and accuracy from my notably illegible longhand.

The publishers are grateful to the following for permission to use illustrations in this book:

Lady Ashcombe: pictures of Sudeley Castle on pp.175, 176, 182.

Ashmolean Museum, Oxford: print of old Richmond Palace, p.155.

Robin Anderson: pictures of Abergeldie Castle on pp.12, 13, 14 and Richmond Palace on pp.150, 151, 152-3, 156-7.

BBC Hulton Picture Library: picture of Arthur, Duke of Connaught, on p.54; view of Clarence House with inset portraits of the Duke and Duchess of Connaught, p.57.

Brighton Pavilion Museum: picture of the Banqueting Room, Royal Pavilion, p.158.

Country Life: picture of Dalkeith House on p.64; ruins of the Medieval Banqueting Hall, Sudeley Castle, p.177; the lake at Sandringham, p.173.

His Grace the Duke of Buccleuch and Marquis of Queensberry KT for the pictures of Drumlanrig Castle on pp.68, 69, 72, 73; the staircase at Dalkeith House, p.65; pictures of Newark Castle on pp.134, 141.

B. Giggins: drawings of Barnwell Castle on pp.31, 33 (reproduced from a survey of Barnwell Castle by the South Midlands Archaeological Society, published by Lammas Publications).

ACKNOWLEDGMENTS

Jarrold & Son Ltd: picture of Barnwell Castle on p.28.

Mansell Collection: drawings of kettle-drums, p.62; horses' heads, p.130; spinning-wheel, p.97; black wolf, p.76.

Mary Evans Picture Library: drawing of ape on p.69; engraving of Drumlanrig Castle, pp.71-2; sketch of Martha Gunn p.162; drawing of David Rizzio, p.111 and reconstruction of the assassination of Rizzio, p.113.

National Portrait Gallery, London: portraits of Anne Boleyn, p.37; Ernest Augustus, Duke of Cumberland, p.167; George II, p.122; George III, p.207; George IV (two portraits), p.162; Lady Jane Grey, p.192; Henry VIII, pp.38, 90; Judge Jeffreys, p.192; Queen Elizabeth I, p.154; Mary, Queen of Scots, p.108; Henrietta Maria, p.142; Catherine Parr, p.178; Margaret Pole, Countess of Salisbury, p.190; Sir Walter Raleigh, p.192; Jane Seymour, p.95; James Scott, Duke of Monmouth, p.66; Henry Stuart, Lord Darnley, p.109; Cardinal Wolsey, p.92. All Crown Copyright.

Press Association: pictures of Althorp Park, p.16; Cortachy Castle, p.58; Nether Lypiatt Manor, p.128; Sandringham, p.170.

PSA Services (Department of the Environment): pictures of Buckingham Palace, p.48; Clarence House, p.52; Hampton Court, pp.94, 100, 103; Kensington Palace, pp.118, 120-121, 123; Tower of London, p.188; Windsor Castle, p.206. All Crown Copyright.

Rex Features: pictures of Gatcombe Park on pp.76, 78-9.

Royal Armouries, Tower of London: picture of sub-crypt at the Tower, p.193. Crown Copyright.

Scottish National Gallery: picture of Archibald, Marquis of Argyll, p.136. Crown Copyright.

Scottish Tourist Board: cover picture of Glamis Castle and another one on p.88; picture of Holyroodhouse on p.116.

David Skinner: picture of colonnades at Queen's House, Greenwich, p.145.

John Steadman: picture of St James's Palace, p.164

George Skipper of Alnwick, for pictures of Bamburgh Castle, Northumberland, on pp.22, 23, 25, 26, 27.

Topham: pictures of Castle of Mey, pp.124, 127.

Woodmansterne Publications/Jeremy Marks: pictures of Blickling Hall on pp.34, 35, 43, 44, 46, 47; Brighton Pavilion on pp.160-1; Glamis on pp.82-3; Hampton Court on title-page and pp.99, 101, 102; Holyroodhouse on pp.105, 106, 107; Queen's House, Greenwich, pp.144, 146-7, 149; Tower of London on pp.183, 184, 185, 189 (top picture), 194, 195, 198, 201, 203; Windsor Castle on pp.204, 205, 206, 208, 209.

INTRODUCTION

It is a cause of alarm in some circles that interest in parapsychology appears to be growing. Mention a branch of this complicated and increasingly scientific subject to almost any group of people, and you will at once have a positive response — positively for or equally positively against whatever aspect of 'psi' you have mentioned.

The interest, I suspect, has always been present in mankind, for there is a mysterious element in life (and even more in death) which drives us to seek explanations for what we fail to understand. In western societies, with their strongly materialistic frameworks, values and expectations, questions without an answer based on these standards make for great insecurity. We *should* be able to explain ghosts, poltergeists, pre– and retrocognition, telepathy, clairvoyance, out-of-body experiences and all forms of extra-sensory perception. After all, are we not logical people with our feet rooted in reality, the reality we see all around us? Ah, yes, no doubt; but it all depends, as a well-known broadcaster used to say, on what you mean by reality. Is the 'reality' we see, touch and hear daily, all there is of the quality? Or is it a great deal larger and stranger than we imagine, and only our limited senses prevent our realizing the bulk of the iceberg beneath its visible tip?

Many of us do sense it, and perhaps at one time all living beings possessed what we now call psychic ability. Animals and young children still seem able to 'see' and 'hear' what the rest of us sophisticated, intellectualized and rational adults are no longer aware of. We live, on the whole, surprisingly narrow lives, consisting of regular routines of working, eating, sleeping and taking a little recreation, and these routines are repeated daily over most of every year after the age of about twenty, until we retire or die. The shepherd boy in the old ballad was so fed-up with sheep-minding and watching nothing but his woolly charges that he was driven to sing: 'There must be something more; there *must* be something more!' There must indeed, and the present book is an attempt to look a little further into what may be under the iceberg's tip in the form of one aspect of 'hidden reality'.

The idea of ghosts and hauntings has been with humanity for most of its existence. Originally, I think, a fear of natural inexplicable occurrences such as thunder, lightning, floods, fires, eclipses, gales, earthquakes, caused man to imagine spirits or gods who governed such things and must be propitiated if humans were to survive. Then there was a second fear, that of death, which swept people from their places in each tiny community, leaving cold clay where there had lately been a living thing. What had become of the dead one? Surely he was nearby — not gone, but merely invisible; or perhaps taken to some special sacred place reserved for such beings. Ultimately the two fears may have coalesced to become the superstitious element which came to fear 'the supernatural'.

Yet now that we are far removed in time and education from this type of superstition, we can see that primitive people may, after all, have been closer to the truth in their simple beliefs than we are in our cynicism. True, natural elements are seen now not as the activities of gods but as expressions of the normal processes of creation. Yet there is something in them still to be respected, uncontrollable as it is by man.

And though the dread of death has abated a little, we, too, are obliged to say that there is some evidence for survival of it. People still see, hear or sense the presence of newly-dead friends or relatives. Scenes from the past do seem to replay occasionally, giving us information about long-gone events and participants. Dead individuals sometimes bring 'messages' or 'warnings' to the living. All these fall into one group. But, and more commonly, there is a second group consisting of petty, meaningless replays of unimportant routines which, like the shepherd boy's sheep, were incredibly boring in life and are no less so after it — the sound of endless sets of footsteps walking down interminable corridors; doors forever opening and closing without benefit of muscle-power; thumpings and bangings which may have meant something in the life of earlier dwellers on the planet, but are now just a sleep-banishing nuisance.

I believe that this 'hidden reality' represents merely another aspect of the way the life force works, and that it is as atomically and scientifically based as everything else in the universe. I do not think it is either *super*natural or *para*normal, but that ultimately it will be found to be as natural as lightning and as normal as thought. This is a theme to which I shall return at the book's end.

In the meantime, why write a book specifically about the royal connection with hauntings? Firstly because of royalty's strong association with major historical events. Royal homes and sites have witnessed some of the most interesting and dramatic happenings on both public and private levels; and it is such events which produce the echoes reverberating so persistently into the future that we call them hauntings. And secondly to disprove the idea that royalty is set apart from the rest of humanity, an élite selected for a superior role in human affairs, which makes its members 'different'; as though they had golden crowns as birthmarks or an innate inability to make errors. People of royal birth are not and never have been superhuman. They share the loves, fears and dreads of the rest of us; and the terms of earthly existence.

Royal homes in this context are broadly interpreted. Not only are specifically royal residences included, but lesser places where the royal connection may be more tenuous and indirect – i.e., possibly by marriage. The royal component, therefore, varies, as does the individual psychic record. That these homes often hold similar records of the smaller folk who served the place is coincidental. All who live leave some trace behind, if only in the memory of others.

ABERGELDIE CASTLE

Aberdeenshire

The little castle of Abergeldie, elegantly perched on the very brink of the River Dee in Aberdeenshire, has never been wholly royal, for it was built for the powerful head of the Gordon clan in the sixteenth century, Sir Alexander Gordon of Midmar, later Earl of Huntly. It was never relinquished, save for a short interlude after the first Jacobite rising, when General Mackay took over and garrisoned Abergeldie in an attempt to defuse the famous Gordon belligerence. The family, undismayed, promptly built Birkhall, until they were able to reclaim their primary castle.

Abergeldie attracted Prince Albert at a time when he was developing his Deeside estate, but his bid for it was declined by the Gordons. However, they agreed to a long lease on a regularly renewable basis, while retaining the freehold. Prince Albert ulti-

The picturesque little castle of Abergeldie, situated on the River Dee (Grampian). It is said to be haunted by the ghost of Kittie Rankie who was burnt as a witch.

opposite
Another view of Abergeldie Castle. Kittie Rankie was burnt on the hilltop overlooking the castle.

13

mately acquired Birkhall, built Balmoral, and allowed members of the Royal Family to use the rented Abergeldie as an alternative summer annexe.

During Queen Victoria's lifetime the Prince and Princess of Wales (the future King Edward VII and Queen Alexandra) annually visited Abergeldie, making it their holiday base in Scotland. And from 1902 to 1910 the little castle was occupied regularly in the summer by the heir to the throne, Prince George (later George V), and his family.

According to Jean Goodman's lively account in *Royal Scotland*, the elder two boys had no escape from the schoolroom even when on holiday, and the future King Edward VIII and the little brother who would one day be George VI, were either kept hard at work by their tutor, or set fiercely difficult mathematical problems by their disciplinarian father. Abergeldie for them was not always a place of beauty and a joy for ever.

However, there were compensations. The young Prince Edward discovered the castle's ghost story.

Abergeldie's dominant architectural feature is a high tower, and in his *Memoirs*, the Prince described it:

> . . . a tall stone tower surmounted by a wooden cupola infested with bats and haunted, we were led to believe, by the ghost of Kittie Rankie, an unfortunate creature who had been burned at the stake as a witch on the hill top overlooking the Castle.

There must have been some truth in the witch-burning story, for Patricia Lindsay, a daughter of the local doctor in the eighteen-fifties, as a child played in one of the castle cellars reputed to have housed poor Kittie in her imprisonment, before she was taken for fiery execution at Craig-na-Ban.

Young Patricia, happy enough to play in the dungeon by day, would not go near it at night, for then (according to the castle's housekeeper, Old Effie) the place might be filled with terrifying noises and the wild mysterious ringing of bells, both symptoms said to augur ill-fortune for the Gordon family.

The two young sons of George V appear not to have heard this version of the ghost story. They were, in any case, fully occupied when not working out — inefficiently and usually incorrectly — the mathematical problems set them by their father, in removing the thin, white, brittle stucco covering the castle's walls. This was a slow process since it needed the application of finger-nails. However, small boys must do something during the day, and it was one way to discover that the castle was, beneath this veneer, built of solid granite.

15

Althorp Park, Northamptonshire, home of the Spencer family since 1508. Its ghosts include a groom, a child, and the 7th Earl.

ALTHORP PARK

Northamptonshire

On 20 July 1639, the beautiful Dorothy Sidney finally married the man she had chosen from her many suitors, to the distress of the poet, Edmund Waller, whose own wooing of her had been unsuccessful. His triumphant rival was Henry Spencer, first Earl of Sunderland, and the wedding was celebrated at the bride's home of Penshurst in Kent. Two years and two children would intervene before the young couple finally settled at Spencer's family seat of Althorp* in Northamptonshire.

There have been Spencers at Althorp Park since the end of the fifteenth century, and all have brought their particular grace and talent to a beautiful house. For this is one of the great English country houses set in the magnificent parkland which has given a sense of happiness and security to many generations of young Spencers, including the present Princess of Wales.

Dorothy Sidney is remembered now chiefly by Waller's love poems to her, *Go, Lovely Rose* and *That which her slender waist confined*; and by his gentle name for her, 'Sacharissa'. Other, later, Spencers would leave different memorabilia, the men frequently becoming engaged in politics and the women marrying into noble families and assuming their traditional roles of aristocratic wives, mothers and hostesses. Always the Spencers seem to have had close relations with the Court, and Althorp has welcomed almost as

* pronounced Alltrop.

16

many generations of royal guests as it has its own lively children.

Robert Spencer, 2nd Earl of Sunderland, had a remarkable gift for staying in political favour in spite of the vicissitudes of Restoration politics, while one of his descendants, that sturdy Viscount Althorp of the 1833 Reform Bill, carved out an honourable political career for himself on a much firmer footing. Of the women, the attractive Sarah, Lady Lyttelton, stands out for her typical Spencer energy and enterprise. Sarah was widowed young, but first found herself Lady of the Bedchamber to Queen Victoria, then latterly Royal Governess to the Queen's large brood of children, to whom she was known affectionately as 'Laddle'. She was at least qualified to teach them arithmetic, for Sarah had herself when young been taught the subject by the famous Edward Gibbon.

Inevitably so fine and old a house as Althorp must have its ghostly echoes. Although it has more than one, perhaps the best known is that of one of its humbler occupants, a groom who had been an especial favourite of his master, George John, the 2nd Earl Spencer, father of Sarah Lyttelton. The single known sighting seems to have occurred some time between 1828 and 1834.

One would expect a groom to haunt, if he haunted at all, the stables, but the attentions of this one were focused on the interior of the house and it was by one of its guests that he was seen.

On one occasion a clergyman, a Mr Drury (later to become Archdeacon), was visiting Althorp and had stayed up late playing billiards with Earl Spencer's son-in-law, Lord Lyttelton. When eventually the two men had had enough of their game and were intending to retire for the night, a servant warned them to be particularly careful to extinguish all lights before going to sleep. The Earl, he added, was keenly aware of fire risks and consequently nervous about the danger to his house and its inhabitants.

Mr Drury, for his part, soon fell asleep, only to be awakened some time later by a very bright light which shone directly into his eyes. For a while he was unable to collect his wits or to understand why he had awakened, and he lay there in the semi-stupified state which often accompanies sudden awakening. Then remembering his whereabouts, he looked up: to see a male figure dressed in a striped shirt and wearing a flat cap, standing at the foot of his bed, steadily regarding him. In its hand the figure held a lighted lantern; it had been the rays from this source falling across his face which had awakened the clergyman.

Drury was puzzled and irritated by this extraordinary invasion, and demanded to know its reason, thinking the house must be on fire at least. His irritation was not dispelled by the intruder's response: absolute silence. The figure continued to regard the clergyman as blankly as though the latter had never spoken. Since the wearing of a dog-collar does not necessarily guarantee saintliness, the cleric was incensed by the insolence of this servant who

17

had so unceremoniously invaded his room and so nonchalantly ignored his questions. In other words, he thoroughly lost his temper and threatened to report the incident to the Earl himself the next morning.

Yet still there was utter silence. The man merely lowered his lantern, still steadily regarding Drury, then turned away and began to walk towards the dressing-room. The clergyman testily called after him that he would not find an exit there, and then — in an extraordinarily strong-minded reaction — turned over and went to sleep, refusing to concern himself any further with the eccentric disturber of his rest.

The following morning he mentioned the matter to his host's daughter, Lady Lyttelton, no doubt still suffering some indignation at the extraordinary behaviour of his nocturnal visitor. He could only think, Drury explained to Sarah, that the man must have been drunk and unaware of what he was doing, although his behaviour had not suggested that of a drunken man.

If Sarah Lyttelton were surprised, she did not show it; in fact she took the matter calmly, merely saying that Mr Drury must have seen her father's favourite groom who, as part of his duties had been required to go the rounds of the house each night in case any careless guest had fallen asleep leaving a light still burning. Where the man was in doubt, he had had instructions to enter bedrooms to make certain such lights were extinguished.

Perhaps Drury raised his eyebrows at the lady's use of the past tense. After all, the groom was still carrying out his master's instruction, was he not?

The answer, as it happened, was in the negative: the groom had died exactly a fortnight before Drury's encounter with him.

One may ask with surprise if it is possible for an individual to carry out, after death, duties which he had conscientiously undertaken in life. Sometimes this appears to occur, whether because the habit of performing certain actions regularly has been able to 'register' on the surroundings and 'replay' itself at intervals; or because the mind's consciousness, surviving physical death, is unable to detach itself from a long-established duty and tries to perpetuate it, is not known.

However it is judged, this Althorp haunting is unusual in that the ghost was of a person very recently dead, who made an appearance not to warn or to say farewell (both common motives for immediate post-death apparitions) but to carry out duties which had been highly meaningful to him in life. Who can tell what luggage we take over with us from our lives? If there is survival, and there is much evidence in its favour, then it seems unreasonable to expect immediate adjustment to the drastic change in circumstances in which the newly-dead finds himself. Time for adaptation is likely to be needed. No doubt Althorp's faithful

18

groom has long since made the transition, for I have not heard of any recent sightings of this phantom.

There have, however, been others, seen by members of the family or the household.

Prior to the First World War, one of the young daughters of the family was in the habit of playing in the house's picture gallery, a place she loved and which had an especial attraction for her. Along one wall of this long room was let in a doorway with an unusually low door; the child herself referred to it (and still does as an adult) as 'the little door'. 'It was', she told me, 'just big enough for a child to enter.'

Several times while playing in the gallery she would draw level with the doorway in time to see a little girl come out of it. She did not recognize the child, and knew that she was not resident in the Althorp of reality. Her clothes alone bespoke her period, for they were of pre-Victorian date, their overall greyness being relieved by darker bands of colour on what appears to have been a tucked bodice. The clothing's appearance — and indeed the child's — was always the same.

There seems no doubt that this phantom child had belonged to the history of Althorp, and certainly several of the eighteenth-century Spencers died in childhood; yet the living Spencer daughter who regularly saw the little ghost failed to recognize her from any of the very many family portraits in the house. Why, one wonders, did she and only she haunt, out of the many who had died as infants through the ages? A tantalizing question. I have a theory (perfectly unprovable) that the ghost child might have been a namesake of the living child, and on that account a bond might have existed between them. This could explain why the one was visible to the other, but not at all why the little grey girl haunted in the first place, or why she did her walking in that particular spot.

The apparition's greyness, incidentally, has probably little to do with the original colour of the clothing. 'Old' phantoms, who have been seen over many decades, possibly centuries, seem to lose colour — if they ever had it in their spectral form — and to appear in monochrome, as black, white or grey, the theory being that more energy is needed to materialize in colour than in monochrome. After such a time lapse, presumably energy is no longer so readily available for the process of materialization. This explanation still holds good, even where the haunting is of the 'recorded/pattern' variety rather than the 'decision-making/spontaneous'.

'A little grey girl in a full-skirted dress — but earlier than the crinoline. . . .' Who else, I wonder, has seen her at Althorp? When passing the real, living child, the phantom never spoke to her, but merely smiled before disappearing. Perhaps what the two children did share — some hundred and fifty years apart — was a love of the rambling beautiful old house to which both belonged.

But there are more recent ghosts at Althorp — or at least one more recent.

Albert Edward John, 7th Earl Spencer, died in 1975. Jack, as he was known to his family and friends, had been a shy man who did not find it easy to relate to people. Perhaps on this account, the love for Althorp which has fired most of the Spencers, burned particularly brightly in him. The house, its contents and its history were his passion, and he made himself so acknowledged an expert that he was asked to serve on several prestigious artistic and antiquarian bodies, including the Wallace Collection and the Victoria and Albert Museum. However, it was not merely beautiful artefacts which Jack Spencer loved, but Althorp itself, its ambience, its grace and its long and evocative history, a history which was in essence the story of himself and his own people.

On Jack's death his son, Edward John ('Johnnie'), inherited title, house and lands, and moved into the family home. His first marriage to Frances Roche, daughter of Lord and Lady Fermoy, had ended in divorce, and their children, Sarah, Jane, Diana and Charles, had chiefly been brought up at Park House on the Sandringham estate, spending only occasional holidays at Althorp. Now Johnnie had re-married, and a wonderfully welcoming family party was in progress at Althorp for him and his new bride, Raine, former Countess of Dartmouth. People streamed through the old house, laughing, talking, and remembering, greeting friends and relatives not seen for months (or years) and filled with the delight of a wholly optimistic occasion.

It is doubtful whether many members of that gathering dwelt on the recent death, or reminded themselves that had it not taken place, their celebrations might have been somewhere other than Althorp. It therefore came as a considerable shock to five of the younger relatives (Spencer cousins and nephews) when on two or three occasions during the course of the party they caught a glimpse of Jack Spencer moving in and with the crowd. He seemed quite at ease and made no acknowledgment to them, though he was smiling. Useless, too, for them to remind themselves that Jack had been dead these many months, for they had seen him there, still at Althorp, walking its beloved rooms, enjoying his house as he always had.

This series of instances is, in itself, extraordinary, but more was to follow. The wife of the butler twice saw her late employer on the stairs, the sightings being preceded each time by a gust of inexplicable hot air. She had been so startled on the first occasion that she had said 'How nice to see you, my lord!', without apparently realizing the nature of the event in which she was taking part. 'Jack' once again had merely smiled and made no reply.

Around this time also, and shortly after the wedding party, a painter decorating one of the house's corridors 'saw' the late Earl walk past him. Again no speech was exchanged, but the man was not unnaturally disconcerted.

Yet again, a member of Jack Spencer's own immediate family felt a strong sense of his presence in the house all through these celebratory days, though without actually seeing him.

It is not unknown for the semblance of dead persons to appear in the area they had occupied in life, such spasmodic appearances often continuing for weeks or even months after death has over-taken them. If it is in truth the human consciousness or energy which survives dissolution of the physical body, what causes its persistence in the scenes known in life? The evidence points to a strong emotion once felt by the living individual which apparently continues to bind him to its object even after death. There are several instances existing of hatred or fear being that binding force, and not a few of its being love.

Jack Spencer's strongest emotion in life would seem to have been for his house. He had deeply loved the place. Perhaps this was where he had been happiest. One can understand his reluctance to leave it.

BAMBURGH CASTLE

Northumberland

It is many centuries since Bamburgh Castle was the seat of the ruler of Britain, yet in its early days it was a royal castle, and has had continual, though intermittent links with royalty from that time.

Bamburgh was built on its great pile of Northumbrian rocks in the sixth century as a fortress in the real sense, for it looked out to sea in the direction from which the invading Angles and Saxons would come — the ultimate English. A British king named Ethelfrith, named it for his wife, Bebba, and 'Bebba's fortress' it was until impatient local tongues shortened it from 'Bebban/burgh' to its present form. It was rebuilt after the Norman Conquest.

Over the centuries it has been captured by Angles, settled in, lost again, held by the Lancastrians against the Yorkists and taken by the latter in 1464, thereafter to change hands several times.

opposite
An interior view of one of the towers in Bamburgh Castle. The portraits are of the Forsters, who owned the castle in the eighteenth century.

23

Its great days, though, were in the time of that vigorous seventh-century saint, Aidan, who converted Oswald, King of Northumbria, to Christianity, and made Bamburgh's walls resound with his preaching. In the eighth century Northumbria itself became renowned throughout Europe as a centre of learning and piety, and when its political decline set in, that reputation still stood unchallenged for several hundred years afterwards.

All England north of the Humber, South-West Scotland and Eastern Scotland to the Firth of Forth: this was the kingdom once ruled from Bamburgh, and its power was formidable.

Now the territory of the castle has dwindled to the acreage of rock on which the building stands, its feet on the escarpment and the sea washing its ankles. In its rejuvenated state, it is a genuine lived-in building, though no longer occupied by one single family. Bamburgh today is divided into apartments, but has lost nothing of its beauty, either without or within the walls.

In most very ancient places one can feel the history stirring. It is as though layer had been laid upon layer, and each vibrated on a different note. Where there are many notes, the visitor — especially the sensitive visitor — often experiences a curious disturbance, as though he were being told several diverse tales at once. Perhaps he is, who knows?

One of Bamburgh's stories is of a ghostly knight whose spectral footsteps resound occasionally in the building. Nothing is known of his life or the period in which he lived.

One woman who occupied a suite of rooms there at the end of the last century, a Miss Sylvia Calmedy-Hamlyn, was related to the then owners of the castle, and her encounter with the Bamburgh ghost was far from reassuring. Miss Calmedy-Hamlyn's quarters were in the twelfth-century keep of the castle, one of the oldest parts of the building. It seems the lady awoke one night to see the 'filmy grey' shape of what appeared to be a knight in full armour, walking across her bedroom floor. Not only did she see the spectre, but also heard it — the distinctive metallic clatter of what she assumed to be chains, though no chains were visible. (Eighty years ago the mere idea of haunting conjured up in the mind's ear the sound of rattling chains; presumably as a mental hangover from the days when prisoners were securely chained to dungeon walls. Destined soon to become ghosts, it was thought prisoners and their fetters must materialize together, thus enabling the spirits to clank hauntingly through the scenes of their earthly gloom.)

opposite
View of the atmospheric interior of Bamburgh Castle. It is easy to imagine this spot being haunted. Note the gleaming eye of the trophy on the wall.

Miss Calmedy-Hamlyn's knight, however, would need no chains to help him clank about the castle; the mere fact that he wore plate armour would have provided enough noise to grace a respectable haunting. In fact, the lady saw (and heard) him both cross her room and walk out into the corridor. Having reached that point, the noise grew even louder as the knight's armoured heels negotiated a

Another view of a tower
in Bamburgh Castle
where a ghostly knight
takes a noctural walk.

Bamburgh Castle, built
on Northumbrian rock.

downward flight of steps; after which they faded into the distance
as he continued his nocturnal walk.

In this, the older part of the castle, armoured knights were
probably a common sight in the thirteenth and fourteenth centuries, the period to which the Bamburgh ghost seems to belong. His
identity is not known, neither is his story, and whatever his reason
for continuing to stalk the halls of mighty Bamburgh, it is unlikely
to come to light.

I do not know of any recent sightings of this ghost.

One of the towers of Bamburgh holds portraits of earlier owners,
the Forsters, an influential border family of the eighteenth century.
This tower is a strongly atmospheric place, and conveys a disturbed
and unhappy impression to the sensitive observer. However, as far
as I know there is no tradition of an actual haunting here. However,
the Forsters were involved in reckless revolutionary activities at
one time, and were to lose one of the family members to the gallows
in consequence of Jacobite commitment. Another of its members,
Dorothy Forster, provides a ghost in her own right, for she is said to
haunt the Lord Crewe Arms at Blanchland.

What truly haunts Bamburgh is probably its very ancientness;
that and the spectacular beauty of its setting. The castle lies,
lionlike, upon its rock and the sea besets it regularly twice daily, as
it has for centuries. St Cuthbert loved this wild land and water so
greatly that later in life he built a hermitage on one of the nearby
Farne Islands to be a prayerful retreat from the struggles of the early
church and kingdom of Britain.

This is indeed an old, old landscape.

BARNWELL CASTLE

Northamptonshire

Not all members of Royal Families own castles, still less live in them. Those who do usually acquire them by inheritance, as with the magnificent pile at Windsor, or by purchase and personal building as with Balmoral's mock-baronial.

Barnwell in Northamptonshire was bought, though not as a dwelling, for it had long been ruined when Prince Henry, Duke of Gloucester, third son of George V, purchased it shortly after his marriage to Lady Alice Montagu-Douglas-Scott. In fact the castle was only a part of the Barnwell estate, and the country home the Duke and Duchess needed they found in Barnwell Manor, a fine Tudor house which looked across its immaculate lawns to the old castle ruins opposite.

Barnwell Castle came into my life in the summer of 1973, when I began researching the hauntings of Northamptonshire, preparatory to writing a book covering the whole of East Anglia — or at least those counties designated by the British Broadcasting Corporation as constituting its East Anglian Region.

It was a local historian, Tom Litchfield, who first told me about Barnwell, for he lived and farmed in the village which had grown up around the castle in the Middle Ages and now existed as a delightful twentieth-century beauty spot in its own right. I should, wrote Tom, find the castle interesting, both on account of its history and because of his own strange experiences there. Vastly intrigued, I drove over to Barnwell to meet him.

Tom, who seemed to know everybody in Northamptonshire with any interest in county history, had kindly approached the royal owner on my behalf and had obtained permission for us both to visit the impressive ruins at Barnwell. But before then he, the historian, and I, the writer, met over a pub lunch to discuss what secrets the castle held. The story Tom Litchfield told me was one of the most extraordinary and alarming tales of haunting I have ever encountered. Also one of the most fascinating.

For years there had been apparently inexplicable occurrences in the neighbourhood of the castle: nothing spectacular, exactly, but oddities. A local policeman patrolling near the castle had encountered 'a rushing wind' on an otherwise windless night. The village postmaster walking his dog near the ruins late one evening had the animal break away from him and run towards the castle. He had hurried after it to bring it under control, and in doing so had come to the southern side of the great ruin when he seemed to be caught in an unexpected gale of wind which swept by him and beyond. He both heard and felt the gust, and immediately afterwards his dog streaked back past him towards the road, her hair bristling. When the postmaster reached home he found his pet waiting on the doorstep, trembling.

An earlier encounter (in the 1930s) had been experienced by yet another police officer, also patrolling the castle precincts. His comment afterwards had been that there was one place in the old castle where he 'wouldn't go for all the tea in China'. The area in question was the ruin's north-east tower. The reputedly 'difficult' areas, then, were the south side of the walls and the north-east tower.

But why were they difficult? Were they haunted? And if so, by what?

Tom Litchfield and an engineer friend of his who had some psychic gifts, had been asking themselves these questions for some time but it was not until 1948 that they took positive action to find answers. The steps proposed, although they actually proved effective were in my opinion, unwise: the friends held a series of ouija séances to try to make contact with the earlier inhabitants of Barnwell Castle.

The séances were three, two held at Litchfield's house in Barnwell, and the third within the actual castle ruins, the precise location being the north-eastern tower of unpleasant reputation. On each occasion, Mr Litchfield made extensive work-notes recording each stage of the proceedings in detail.

The first of these attempts took place on 20 September 1948, and as with most sessions of this type, an immediate contact appears to have been made, with in this case a respondent purporting to be a sometime Abbot of Ramsey Abbey. The castle, 'he' announced, had in the fourteenth century been used as a court of justice and summary execution; a fact which was later verified by Tom Litchfield from ancient records of the abbey concerned.

However, the mention of execution produced an alteration in the respondent's identity. The next answers to questions were markedly more elaborate and archaic in form and seemed to come from a woman. In reply to the obvious question, the response was that 'she' was 'Marie, uxor (wife) of Le Moyne'. (The castle had probably been completed by Bervengarius Le Moyne in 1266.) Earlier this respondent referred to 'horror and untimely death', and now Tom Litchfield asked for further explanation. The replies were succinct and to the point. The horror and death referred, said the respondent, to a chest in the dungeon, and therein lay the remnants of a ruined life. When asked to whose life she referred, the reply came back immediately: 'Mine. Marie uxor Le Moyne'. This death had taken place when the castle was still in the process of being built.

Then the inquirers put forward a key question: 'How was your life ruined?' The answer: 'By heathen rule enforcing a brutish captivity.' By this time the questioners felt themselves on the brink of an extraordinary discovery, and asked who it was who had imprisoned this unhappy wife. But they were not to be told. All 'she' would say was: 'Secret. I can never betray my soul's secret.' And that was as far as they could go. The respondent's only other comment was that it had been a terrible death. 'He came quietly. Play not for time, he will win the race.'

At this high — and eerie — point in the investigation, the communications petered out. Later Tom Litchfield discovered by diligent research that one of the Le Moyne lords had had a wife named Marie; and that a local legend credited a Le Moyne (Berengarius, son of Richard, the castle's builder) with walling up a woman alive into the uncompleted castle. And, if further substantiation were needed, it was found to be factually correct that Marie Le Moyne had died during the building of the castle.

So far, so intriguing. The second séance was held on 30 September 1948, in the same house. Reginald Le Moyne was the first communicator, but he almost at once handed over to one Berengarius Le Moyne, whom he dubbed his successor, and called, mysteriously, 'the second bastion'.

With Berengarius the inquirers got more than they bargained for,

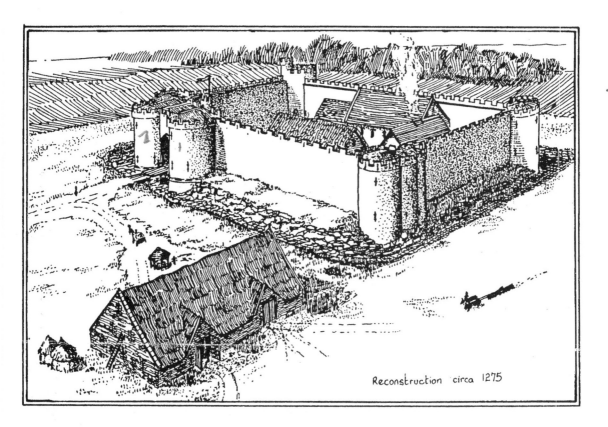

Reconstruction circa 1275

for when 'he' was asked the major question plaguing the minds of his interrogators: 'What is there in the left bastion*?', the reply came back with some power: 'The horrid remnants of suppression which befell an honest lord. William forced my reason.'

William? Who on earth was William? 'We call him covert in Ramsey,' replied the respondent.

William, on later inquiry, turned out to be Abbot William of Godmanchester, contemporary with Berengarius Le Moyne. It was this prelate, noted for his tight-fistedness with money, who had compelled Berengarius to cede the castle and its lands back to the Abbey, though whether because the Le Moynes had illegally seized church lands, or whether as some dire form of penance is not known. Berengarius was apparently claiming in the séance that his mind had become unhinged by the undue pressure applied to him.

The last of the three séances was to be held in the north-eastern tower of the castle itself, and on the night of 9 November 1948, the ouija paraphernalia was set up on a flat stone slab within the tower itself. Since the night was of the soft, black, damp and dense kind in

A reconstruction of Barnwell Castle as it appeared in the thirteenth century. (Drawing by B. Giggins.)

* Barnwell Castle possesses three bastions at its main gate rather than the usual two.

31

which November specializes, a storm lantern was placed beside the stone table. The session lasted only a few minutes but was hair-raising.

Contact was immediately established with Berengarius Le Moyne, and in response to a question asking him what he wished to say, there was a *non sequitur* of a reply.

'I will fire to warn you.'

At once above and behind the inquirers' heads came the sharp crack of a handgun or of a whip. When the two men turned, they looked straight at the head and upper body of a monk, poised in the doorway to the main courtyard. At that point, their nerve broke and they raced from the tower.

Some time later Mr Litchfield, still curious, but no longer desirous of pursuing the ouija investigation, visited All Saints Church at Sawtrey near Barnwell, where he knew the Le Moyne family were commemorated. Here he found the customary memorial brass tablet, but above it was an insignia of the Le Moynes. It was in the form of the upper torso of a monk; in his hand he carried a folded whip.

Now the parapsychological elements present in the ouija sessions came together startlingly with the physical, circumstantial proof: the 'coincidence' of the two Maries Le Moyne; the details of Berengarius's loss of his property to Abbot William; the identification of ghostly monk and whip with the actual symbol monk with whip (about which the inquirers appear to have been unaware at the time of the second séance). And then the mystery of the gate bastions. Why were there *three* bastions in this castle rather than the customary two? Why the third, and what purpose was it built to serve? Could this be the site of the missing castle dungeon? And, if so, is that dungeon perhaps a secret room contained by the extraordinarily thick wall of this bastion? Most of the *psi* occurrences outside the castle walls seem to have been in this vicinity. The 'rushing wind' certainly occurred near the gatehouse.

And if the second left-hand bastion does hold a secret room built into its wall, is there any trace of a prisoner who might have been shut up within it and left to starve to death? A woman prisoner, once named Marie Le Moyne.

The answers to such questions are unlikely to be known unless at some time in the future an owner of Barnwell Castle should demolish the far left bastion of its historic gatehouse. The castle's royal owners will, I imagine, leave the beautiful medieval ruin to moulder in peace, as it has for the last seven hundred years. No purpose would be served by interfering with the slow processes of nature, other than to give a skeleton — if such exists within the bastion — a consecrated burial.

The corollary to this extraordinary story is that at least one of the two inquirers seems to have felt its effects for the rest of his life.

When I was in conversation with Tom Litchfield only a few weeks before his death in 1985, he seemed then to wish that he had not investigated the castle's secret. The memory of its circumstances had not left him during the intervening years. He was a good and sensitive man, and too intelligent not to know that he might have been happier without a knowledge of this particular grim piece of thirteenth-century history and its disturbing temporal echoes.

My personal feeling about the use of ouija (the arrangement of the alphabet around a circular table and the use of an ordinary tumbler as a pointer to its letters), is that it should not be undertaken in any circumstances. The inexperienced tend to regard it as a kind of parlour or party game, which assuredly it is not. Neither, though, is it a form of childish superstition, totally harmless and often amusing in its results. The fact is that the use of the pointer — or rather the fact that several persons combine to place their fingers upon the tumbler — appears to generate a group power, which does not seem to be under the control of either the group as a whole or any individual member of it. The result can be at its best alarming and at its worst terrifying.

Since we have not yet reached the state of knowledge where we understand the nature of such power or its means of generation or control, to 'play' with it as though it were a form of tiddly-winks is both foolhardy and irresponsible. It is just possible the force may turn out to be a fundamental natural one, with possibly destructive properties if misapplied. Does one allow toddlers to play with naked electric wires? Not if one wishes to see them reach maturity.

Similar strictures to these may also apply to all forms of séance. Knowledge (of the parapsychological or any form of *psi*) is best bequeathed or involuntarily acquired. To demand it, to hammer on heaven's gates and insist on having it, may ultimately not be in our own best interests. Perhaps if experience teaches anything, it is that information comes to each human exactly when he is ready and able to handle it.

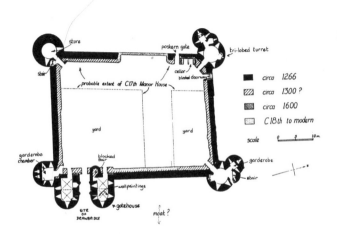

Ground plan of Barnwell Castle. (Drawing by B. Giggins.)

South front of Blickling Hall, Norfolk, associated with Anne Boleyn, whose ghost is said to haunt it. Other ghosts include a headless rider and a coach drawn by headless horses.

BLICKLING HALL

Norfolk

I saw the house for the first time after I had lived in Norfolk for three months. Before then I had not even known of Blickling's existence. It is arguably the most beautiful small manor house in England. It stands far back from the road, carefully sheltered on two sides by ancient and imposing yew hedges (trimmed to a whisker, and twice as tall as a man) with the minor arms of its buildings reaching around from beyond the filled-in moat to touch the giant wall of hedge.

The house itself is symmetrical, offering an elegantly balanced outline of towers and chimneys against the high Norfolk skies. But it is the colour which surprises, for the bricks are a warm rose-red and the old house glows like a garnet. From the road one can almost but not quite see the stone bulls which guard the house entrance. Bulls that some say are the emblems of the Hobarts, who owned the house from the seventeenth century and who were responsible for

erecting the present fine Jacobean building on the site of a medieval structure.

Other experts are equally certain that the bulls guarding the house speak for its earlier owners, the Boleyns or Bullens, whose fortunes rose meteorically from humble beginnings and fell with the same astral speed into extinction.

Thomas Boleyn's grandfather's name had been spelled plain Bullen, and this was not unsuitable for one who earned his living in trade, although 'living' is understating the case, for old Bullen was a wool and silk merchant (or, more precisely, a mercer) and soon amassed considerable wealth. He became Lord Mayor of London, married into the aristocracy and produced a son. The merchant's son caught the attention of a powerful Norfolk magnate, Sir John Fastolf, large in body, heart and character as well as property (Fastolf was to be one of the two originals on which Shakespeare based his Falstaff). Fastolf owned the medieval manor of Blickling, near Aylsham, and the small manor house at its centre, and when he died he willed the property to his protégé, young Bullen.

It was this young man who married a daughter of Lord Ormonde.

East front of Blickling Hall, showing the gardens. The lake is on the extreme right.

35

And it was his son, Thomas, grandson of the mercer, who spelled his name Boleyn and inherited Blickling.

Thomas and Elizabeth Boleyn (he had prudently married into the noble Howard family) had three children, Mary, George and Anne, and all three travelled further afield than was usual for the time. Mary and Anne both spent a part of their childhood and adolescence at the French court, as small maids-in-waiting and George was to visit Italy and France as a young man. Mary acquired a reputation for easy virtue and a succession of French protectors. On her return to England, however, she caught the roving eye of its young King, and despite the fact that she had now also married, she became Henry VIII's mistress, remaining so for six years.

Then her sister, Anne, came to court. Anne was of harder stuff than the compliant Mary. She had, in any case, already fallen in love with a boy of her own age, young Percy, heir of the great northern Earl of Northumberland, and the two planned to marry. Private arrangements were not the custom among public figures, however, and the King and his minister Wolsey had intended that Anne should be a political pawn, as was suitable for a well-born young girl. Wolsey forced Percy into a marriage elsewhere and Anne was pressured to wed an Irish notable. When she refused point-blank to obey, she was packed off to her home castle of Hever as an exile from the Court. It was many months before she returned, and when she did the King first really looked at her. After that, his ageing wife, Catherine, and his mistress, Mary, ceased to exist for him. He wanted Thomas Boleyn's younger daughter and meant to have her.

The rest is a familiar story. Anne would not take over her sister's role, feeling that the King owed her something for wrecking her earlier marriage plans with Percy; feeling, too, that she was of value in herself and not to be treated as a purchasable object. If the King wanted her — and she was now beginning to find him attractive, for he was in the prime of his manhood and still handsome and athletic — then he must marry her. Henry, for his part, and for the first time in his life, had fallen deeply in love. Being accustomed to instant gratification of his wishes, he could not accept that this wayward, spirited young girl was out of reach. He intended to have her if he had to remake the kingdom in order to do it. And that virtually was what he did, for the divorce from Catherine of Aragon, his loyal wife of many years, was gained only at the expense of tearing the country from the Roman Catholic church and religion and pushing it into another, 'reformed' version of Christianity, with the King at its head rather than the Pope. Henry's falling in love altered the entire course of history for his people.

In due course, the King divorced his wife and married Anne Boleyn, though not to live happily ever after. For Henry wanted a son, the King needed a son, and the Kingdom needed an heir. Queen Catherine's only living child had been female, the Princess

Anne Boleyn, second wife of Henry VIII (artist unknown).

38

Mary; and females were useful only as political pawns not as heirs to a great throne. Anne's expected child must be, *had* to be a boy. Yet on 7 September 1533, the new Queen gave birth to a useless girl, who was to be called Elizabeth after the mother of each of her parents. Henry's dismay and grief were only equalled by Anne's. The King's ardour began to cool a little. Soon he started to look elsewhere and his eye fell upon a woman the exact opposite of his vibrant, mercurial, ambitious new Queen. Jane Seymour was quiet, demure, undemanding and adoring. Henry began to frequent Wolf Hall in Wiltshire as he had once frequented Hever Castle.

Anne, however, was pregnant again and full of hope for a son. The relations between King and Queen briefly improved, only to disintegrate when the birth took place. The child was the hoped-for boy, but was stillborn.

After that nothing was left but ashes, and Anne, on the pretext of having cuckolded the King with five men, including her brother, and thus committed treason, was arrested and confined to the Tower. All five accused, plus the Queen, were found guilty of the trumped-up crimes charged to them and sentenced to death. The men were executed first; the Queen was to die on 18 May, but had requested death by the sword rather than the axe, and delay took place while an expert executioner with this weapon was brought from Calais. Therefore it was on the morning of 19 May 1536 that Anne Boleyn walked out to the low dais on the little square of green within the walls of the Tower of London. She wore a simple grey damask robe, trimmed with fur, and a pearl-trimmed headdress. Her last sight on earth must have been the adjacent Chapel of St Peter ad Vincula, in which her brother's body already lay and in which she would join him.

This, then, is the story of Anne Boleyn, who as a child (according to tradition) spent occasional holidays at Blickling Hall, with her parents, brother and sister.

And what of this tradition? What proof is there that the child, Anne, ever visited this sylvan, secure retreat? Not much, actually, though there is equally no proof to the contrary, and one relies on the strength of local legend, plus the presence of two or three artefacts, to tip the scales towards the likelihood of her having visited Blickling often as a young child. In one of the rooms of the present Hall there is a wooden plaque dated circa 1780, which states that she was born at Blickling; and in another is a pole screen enclosing a piece of infinitely frail material which is reputed to have belonged to her bedcover. Fragile links with the past, indeed; but tradition often contains more than a germ of truth.

The third link in the chain is even more tenuous, for it is a poem said to have been written by Anne during her imprisonment in the Tower. In the rough fashion in which it has so far appeared in print, it bears only a thin resemblance to poetry:

opposite
Henry VIII as a young man (artist unknown).

A captive, I in this dread Tower, scenes of childhood recall,
They comfort bring in this dark hour now gaiety hath flown.
Through Blickling glades I fain would ride, soft green sward,
Sequestered shade, no cruel intrigues to deride my simple rustic
    day.
A child, I watched the timid fawn, gentle-eyed, steal to the lake
With thirst to quench when mists of dawn had from cool waters
    fled.
Strutting peacocks, shimmering blue, roseate arbour, scented walk;
Gladly I left, 'tis strangely true, for pageantry at Court,
False vanities my pride hath tricked, this place of dank and
    anguished stone
By sullen river surges licked, doth mock my hopeless lot.
Oh, were I still a child in stature small
To tread the rose-lined paths of Blickling Hall.

This is such poor poetry by the standards of her time that one is at first inclined to disbelieve that Anne had anything to do with it; it appears, in fact, more like the attempt of a non-poet of Victorian times to fabricate a piece of evidence. Yet is it? Could one brought up in the cultured Court of France, subject to the beginnings of the Renaissance, as Anne Boleyn was, have perpetrated this piece of non-rhyming, unrhythmical, formless doggerel? Even her royal lord wrote better verse than this.

But, since the thing is purporting to be evidence for Anne's connection with Blickling, let us look at it again. And this time, rearrange the lines.

> A captive, I, in this dread Tower,
> Scenes of childhood recall,
> They comfort bring in this dark hour
> Now gaiety hath flown.
> Through Blickling glades
> I fain would ride,
> Soft green sward,
> Sequestered shade,
> No cruel intrigues to deride
> My simple rustic day.
> A child, I watched the timid fawn,
> Gentle eyed, steal to the lake,
> With thirst to quench when mists of dawn
> Had from cool waters fled.
> Strutting peacocks, shimmering blue,
> Roseate arbour, scented walk;
> Gladly I left,
> 'T'is strangely true,
> For pageantry at Court.

False vanities my pride hath tricked;
This place of dank and anguished stone
By sullen river surges licked,
Doth mock my hopeless lot.
Oh were I still a child in stature small,
To tread the rose-lined paths of Blickling Hall.

Still not great poetry, but now more spontaneous, immediate and moving; the kind of jumbled memories a woman in her situation might have recorded. I suspect, even now, that the verses may have been doctored by Victorian tinkerers, but one phrase at least rings true. 'By sullen river surges licked'. Only someone who had lived in the Tower and seen the tidal Thames flood through the watergates twice daily to lap the area between inner and outer walls still known (though dry now) as Water Lane; someone who had seen the great green moat brim-full with the surging spring tides — only such an individual could have written that poignant phrase.

As for the rest, who knows? I am inclined to think that these may indeed have been Anne's jottings. If they were, then there is no doubt that she knew Blickling very well.

Once Anne Boleyn was dead, and before the resulting shudder of horror which ran through the nerves of her countrymen had subsided, stories began to be told of strange happenings in Norfolk in the Blickling neighbourhood. A coach drawn by headless horses had galloped to the door of Blickling Hall, and inside sat the form of a young woman, headless, too, with the bleeding head upon her lap. For good measure, the horseman, also, was headless. As the years went by, the apparition was said to repeat its appearance on the anniversary of her death, 19 May, accompanied by a red glow from within the coach, and an eerie blue light following it. Occasionally, there was a varied report or two: the coach was driven by Sir Thomas Boleyn, Anne's father. Or the coach dragged behind it a headless male corpse, thought to be that of her brother, George Boleyn, Lord Rochfort. As the years passed, countryfolk embroidered the legends a bit. The coach was pursued by screaming devils; it was fated to cross forty bridges in its headlong journey; or twelve bridges.

Tradition has it that Anne's ghost has been seen gliding about the house's corridors, though the present Jacobean building was not erected until nearly a century after her death. It dates from 1616 to 1627. This need not invalidate any genuine haunting by the ill-fated Queen, since it is not uncommon for active ghosts of a building on an old site to transfer themselves to one replacing it. Sometimes it seems as if it is the site itself rather than the particular building which is haunted.

One would expect the occupants of Blickling Hall and those who have long worked in it to be nearer to the truth of the place than those merely visiting as tourists; and so it proves. Mr Steve Ingram, the present Administrator, told me of a curious experience of his own which occurred in 1985.

He and his wife have a flat in the Hall, and on the night in question Mr Ingram, normally a heavy sleeper, was awakened suddenly at about 1.30 a.m. by the sound of footsteps coming down the passageway leading towards the Ingrams' bedroom. He was not in a half-asleep state, but had come fully wide awake, with all his senses alert, and what he heard was interesting. It was the sound of light female footsteps walking initially on rushmatting (with which, incidentally, the relevant corridor is covered), whose sound then changed to that of someone walking on a thinner, lighter material for a couple of steps, altering in turn to that of the sounds of shoes on carpet. Then the sound stopped. And Steve Ingram knew the walker was in the bedroom. (The lighter sound was due to a thin mat by the room's entrance, which then gave way to a thicker carpet.) What is more, he knew where the walker was now standing: exactly at the foot of the Ingrams' bed on the side occupied by his wife. Steve was not disposed to worry about any of this, for he was convinced that his wife had got up to go to the bathroom and was now returning to bed. So he switched on the bedside light.

His wife, as it happened, was sound asleep on her side of the bed, the bedroom door was shut and no one stood at the bed's foot.

Needless to say, the Administrator related this unnerving incident to his colleagues the following morning, when it was pointed out to him that the previous day had been 19 May, the anniversary of Anne Boleyn's execution. The occurrence has so far not been repeated.

Mr Denis Mead, a former Custodian of the Hall, and still with a finger on its pulse, told me of an event in which an old retainer of the house had been involved. Blickling Manor passed from the Boleyn kin finally in 1616, when it was purchased by a Sir Henry Hobart, and with this family or its lateral branches it remained until bequeathed to the National Trust in the present century. When the Trust took over fully in 1946 (Blickling had been in the occupation of the RAF during the Second World War), it also retained the services of five former employees, including a Mr Sidney Hancock, former butler to the previous owner, Lord Lothian. Dennis Mead described Hancock as a very practical man and not at all imaginative, so that when the latter looked out of a small kitchen window of the Hall towards the lake and saw a woman walking down to the water, he assumed she was either a visitor who had lost her bearings or an intruder trespassing. He noted that she was somewhat unusually dressed, wearing a long grey gown with a white lace collar and a white mob cap, but no doubt attributed this to eccentricity or a vagary of the New Look which was then sweeping

The Chinese Bedroom, Blickling Hall. Several of the bedrooms are said to be haunted.

post-war Britain. In any case, he did not allow it to deter him, and went towards the woman to find out her purpose in being where she was. According to Hancock's own account afterwards, he asked if he might help her, and if she were looking for someone. The reply was more enigmatic than enlightening.

'That for which I seek has long since gone.'

Puzzled by this response, the phlegmatic Hancock turned his head for a moment to look at the house, then back to reply to the stranger. But there was no stranger. He was totally alone by the lakeside. At that moment, he was certain that what had addressed him was not of flesh and blood.

In my conversation with Denis Mead I questioned the assumption that the phantom may have been that of Anne Boleyn, on the grounds of costume. 'It sounds', I said, 'more like that of the next century than of hers, the sixteenth.' But he assured me that Anne went to the scaffold wearing a costume of precisely this description. Francis Hackett, however, in his lively biography, *Henry VIII*, describes Anne's apparel on that final morning as being a grey damask dress, fur-trimmed and low cut with a dark red undergown beneath it. Her head was covered by a small pearl-embroidered headdress with a net attached to keep her hair from falling on to her neck. A significant touch, that last.

43

The Long Gallery,
Blickling Hall.

Yet, it must be remembered that Anne's execution was to have
been on 18 May, and had been delayed by a day in order to secure a
swordsman-executioner. What was she wearing on the fearful day
before she died? Grey dress, white collar, white mob cap? It seems
not unlikely.

But apart from the tragic Anne, who else haunts Blickling? More
than one previous inhabitant, it seems.

Before the National Trust assumed full responsibility for the property, it was let to tenants, and at one period shortly after the Second World War the first floor flat was occupied by a family with two sons, one of whom, Peter, celebrated his twenty-first birthday during their tenancy. On the morning of his birthday, the young man, deciding to play a practical joke on his parents, donned one of the suits of armour in the house and clanked along to their bedroom around dawn, waking them to the sound of a mailed fist hammering on their door. What reception he received is not recorded.

Sadly young Peter died tragically the following year, the family moved away and the flat was then let to another tenant who knew nothing of the previous occupants. This second tenant kept a manservant, and on one occasion said to him: 'You were up early this morning, weren't you?' The man, surprised, denied the fact, saying that he had actually overslept; which was puzzling to his employer who had been awakened around dawn by the sound of very heavy footsteps walking down the corridor outside his bedroom. The subject was then discussed with guests who were sleeping in the house, and had also been awakened early that morning by the same noise. One likened it to 'the sound made by a man dressed in armour'. At which point there was general laughter at such a ludicrous idea.

Later the tenant mentioned the matter to one of the old Blickling servants and to Denis Mead. The armour reference did not surprise them, for the date of the mysterious walking was the precise anniversary of young Peter's birthday.

In my conversations with the Blickling staff several references were made to the south-west tower as an area which had stories attached to it. The bedroom there had once been that of a seventeenth-century owner, Sir Henry Hobart, the 4th Baronet who died in 1698 following a duel a few miles away, arising from a political quarrel. His opponent, Oliver le Neve, was a left-handed swordsman, and easily out-manoeuvred Sir Henry, running him through the body and mortally wounding him. Hobart is said to have died in the south-west tower bedroom at Blickling.

While there is no sound evidence of a haunting in this room, one of the original servants, Mr Leslie Newstead, a man of down-to-earth practicality, had often sensed a presence there — that familiar feeling of not being alone in a room, when one patently is. A mildly supportive testimony was afforded by a former Administrator, Major-General Philip Tower, whose dog would never go willingly into this particular room, but would stand on the threshold, whining and snarling, and with its hackles up.

This suspicion of haunting was put to the test during the Air Force's wartime occupation of Blickling, when the room was allotted to the Commanding Officer of the unit billeted there. He slept in it for one night and moved out again next morning, complaining that he was unable to make any of the three doors stay

South Drawing Room, Blickling Hall.

closed. As fast as he had shut them they had opened again, in spite of the fact that the locks appeared to be in perfect working order. One night of that was enough, apparently. As far as is known, nothing has actually been seen in the south-west tower bedroom, so the evidence, though possibly indicative of a haunting, is inconclusive.

One of the present staff does not like or feel comfortable in the small bedroom (known as the 'O' bedroom) which leads off the print room. She is unable to explain the sensation, but always encounters it when she enters this bedroom, and finds herself leaving it as quickly as possible. When I went into the 'O' room and stayed for a few minutes, I thought there was a 'dead' spot near the bedhead, between it and the wall — dead in the sense that dampness is 'dead', with no sensation of life passing through it. However, nothing is known of this room, and there seems no reason for it to feel unpleasant.

The only other phenomenon encountered at Blickling relates to the south drawing room (the original 'Great Chamber'), a handsome, well-proportioned and dignified room on the first floor through which tourists regularly pass when visiting the house. Some few years ago, a member of the then staff was leaving and a party in his honour was being held in this room. The jollification

was in full swing, when the public relations officer of the time chanced to look up, his eye being drawn to a certain corner of the room, flanked on one side by windows and on the other by the dark painted canvas which covers the walls. He was astonished to see a male figure appear there, dressed in historic fashion. Unfortunately, the PRO no longer lives in the region and could not therefore be interviewed, so no further information is available on the details of this apparition. One assumes it behaved as such materializations usually do, disappearing quite soon after the sighting took place. Some of the old servants of the Hall told Denis Mead of a cook who had worked in the house and had kept a pet cat. Exploring, as cats love to do, the animal somehow found its way into the extensive attics and became lost there. It was not found, in spite of searches, and it was only when over the next few years the persistent mewing of a cat was heard coming from the attics that the truth was guessed. So this is one more 'ghost' — an audible, animal one — to add to the several echoes of the past which survive in Blickling. But without doubt, it is the long-dead Queen who is best remembered there.

Do we survive death? Apparently some of us may. And if the links with earth are strong enough, perhaps sometimes we are able to return to the old, loved, lost places.

Buckingham Palace, London. The sound of a gunshot has been heard in a first-floor office, where a private secretary shot himself, and the ghost of a monk has been seen walking along the terrace overlooking the Palace gardens.

BUCKINGHAM PALACE

London

Although Buckingham Palace is not the most alluring of Royal dwellings, lacking the dominant presence of Windsor Castle, the Victorian dream-quality of Balmoral or the comfortable country solidity of Sandringham, it is undoubtedly an imposing building and much beloved of tourists and addicted royalty-watchers. For at least the last hundred years it has seemed the epitome of monarchical rule, the one stable point in a world where thrones fell, eminent personages were assassinated and national frontiers redrawn overnight. The palace was The Palace. It was inconceivable that the sovereign's flag should not continue to fly from its standard and that the Royal Family's lives should not be conducted behind its closed doors.

Such was not always the case, though, for the building had originally been plain Buckingham House, built by John Sheffield,

Duke of Buckingham, in the reign of Queen Anne. Not until George III occupied the throne of England did the building come into royal ownership. The King purchased it and during the two succeeding reigns its simple elegant frontage was metamorphosed into the elongated outline which distinguishes the present building. There were a number of hiccups in the process, for George IV, never a parsimonious monarch, ran into financial difficulties with what were known as 'the renovations', and his architect, Nash, seems to have had second and third thoughts on what should be done, before arriving at final bricks and mortar. By the time Buckingham House had been re-named Buckingham Palace, it had lost what beauty it once possessed and become merely functional with, to quote the architectural critic W.H. Leeds, a deficiency 'in grandeur and nobleness of aspect'. George IV never lived in the place, and his brother, William IV, who succeeded him, made no secret of his hatred of it, in spite of the fact that he had been born within its walls.

William, fervently hoping he would never have to live in 'the New Palace' as it was originally called, seized an apparently heaven-sent chance in 1834 when the Houses of Parliament burned down, by offering the parliamentarians Buckingham Palace as a new home and a permanent gift from the Crown. The Government, much to the King's annoyance, declined, having heard enough rumours about the place's disadvantages to discourage them from accepting the offer. William had no alternative but to occupy the house himself.

However, he never actually reached it, for what with endless delays and hitches with the restoration and the King's rapidly declining health, it was May 1837 before the palace was ready to receive its new royal owner. And by that time William was beyond moving. He died in Windsor Castle in June of the same year, and that great white elephant, the palace, devolved upon his successor.

As it happened, the young Queen Victoria raised no demur about living in it, and the surrounding area which had until then been rather squalid, rapidly acquired status. She was to spend most of her married life within its walls and to rear her large family of children there. The memory of the happy times they had enjoyed together made the palace unbearable after the Prince Consort's death, and the widowed Queen came less and less often to it as her life proceeded.

Victoria died on 22 January 1901, and her son, Bertie, became Edward VII. He at once set about brightening up what he referred to as 'the sepulchre'. Thereafter, the King conducted his life against the palace's background, and his somewhat raffish court must have formed a striking contrast to that of his mother. He died there just before midnight on 6 May 1910 and the palace and its throne passed to his heir and second son, George V. It was to see its royal owners

49

through two World Wars and the abdication of George V's heir, Edward VIII, who had, incidentally, little love for Buckingham Palace. He thought it smelled damp and musty and he spent most of his time as King in his private residence, Fort Belvedere, where he was able to entertain his own friends freely. Among them was Mrs Wallis Simpson, his future wife, whose reaction to Nash's great building was not encouraging.

On one occasion the King and Mrs Simpson were expected at the palace for dinner at 8.30, and the punctilious staff had everything ready for serving at precisely that time. However, the clock hands crept round to nine o'clock, then to ten with no sign of the royal host and his guest. Finally, at 10.30 the pair arrived, and the kitchen staff, with a dinner now just about in ruins, thought to begin serving. However, the King's friend felt that certain of the large ornaments in the dining-room needed urgent re-arranging, and what was dinner compared with that? She proceeded to order footmen to move the ornaments from one place to another until they should suit her taste. All of which took an unconscionable time, with the result that it was almost midnight before the weary servants could deal with the meal which was their main task of the evening.

One would expect that any paranormal echoes might be of the unhappiness of this period, but there is no record of any such.

There are, however, rumours of two ghosts in the palace. The first is of ancient origin, for it relates to the time when the house's grounds were monastic property. The beautiful pleasure gardens now known as St James's Park were originally low-lying, marshy land extending from the boundary of the present Buckingham Palace on one side to the site of what is now St James's Palace on the other. Somewhere in between stood a leper hospital of St James the Less, patron saint of lepers, leprosy having made its appearance in England in the train of the invading Normans. For a while the dread disease was a scourge and leper hospitals appeared in various parts of the country, run by the religious organizations of the time. That of St James the Less was one such, originally staffed by monks and later by nuns for female patients. Eventually, when the incidence of leprosy lessened, the land and its buildings became the property of the Crown, being purchased by Henry VIII from the Provost of Eton.

It might be thought that echoes of its monastic past would long since have faded from the area, but it is apparently not so. The ghost of a monk has been seen walking along the grand terrace overlooking the palace gardens, and his appearances seem to occur only on Christmas Day each year. The monk in his lifetime must have been a prisoner in his own Priory, for his spirit, when seen, is bound in chains and clanks miserably as it moves. J.A. Brooks, who quotes this sighting, states that the ghost's original died in the

Priory's punishment cell. This may possibly be true, for the early medieval religious orders were not noted for leniency towards their offending members. Any monk or nun caught contravening the laws was likely to be built into the convent/priory walls before he could even utter a plea for mercy. Pleas for mercy, in any case, were not thought highly of at the time. However, this particular monk is one of the anniversary haunting type, and it is probable he may have died on a Christmas Day many centuries ago. Only the original monastery records could give the facts in this case, and these were doubtlessly destroyed at the time of the Dissolution.

Buckingham Palace's second ghost is of fairly recent origin. In the early part of the present century, a certain Major John Gwynne was private secretary to King Edward VII. The unfortunate man became involved in a divorce case, and the resulting scandal and the social ostracism typical of the period apparently proved too much for him, for he retired into his first-floor office and blew out his brains with a revolver. Since then the sound of the gun's report is said to be heard from time to time in the neighbourhood of the room concerned.

One would have expected echoes of the restless Edward VIII perhaps, or of his brother George VI, who was so unwillingly pushed into responsibilities for which he had neither desire nor training, to linger physically in the palace's great rooms, but this does not seem to have occurred. Neither man liked Buckingham Palace, which may account for an absence of desire to return there. The new young Royal Family of George VI was to grow into its position with grace and dignity and to act as a talisman to a nation about to endure a second horrific World War. When the King tragically died of cancer in 1952, the nation felt unfairly deprived of the good shy man they had come to respect and love. His presence was gone from them, though possibly not — at least initially — from his grieving family. He died, as it happened (and as he would have wished it) not in the chilly reaches of Buckingham Palace, but at his beloved Sandringham in Norfolk.

overleaf
**Clarence House, London.
The ballroom is
associated with psychic
phenomena.**

CLARENCE HOUSE
London

'Our Court of St James' ', which is still the official title accredited to foreign ambassadors to England, originally referred to the fact that the sovereign (and by implication, his government) was based at St James's Palace.

The palace itself was built on the site of a former leper hospital by Henry VIII, and with his usual eye to convenience as well as beauty, he had the great marshy expanse surrounding it suitably drained and turned into one of London's finest pleasure gardens, St James's Park. Fittingly for a hunting monarch, he stocked it with deer, and limited the enjoyment of the park's pleasure-giving properties to the sovereign and members of his Court.

St James's itself has an intricate history, with a startling haunting to throw light on a little of it; less lurid, but no less unusual, is the story told of Clarence House, which adjoins the old palace itself.

It was built fairly late in time (1825) for William IV before his accesssion to the throne. His then title, Duke of Clarence, named the house. In turn it became the home of the mother of Queen Victoria, the Duchess of Kent; and of the Queen's second son, the Duke of Edinburgh, who in turn passed it to his younger brother, Arthur, Duke of Connaught. Later it became the official residence of HM Queen Elizabeth II before she acceded, and the home variously of HM Queen Elizabeth the Queen Mother and of HRH Princess Margaret.

It is a fine, dignified old house, though it has gone through periods of common occupation; such as the period during the Second World War when it was taken over and used by the British Red Cross Society's Foreign Relations Department.

It is to this period in its history that the account of the haunting belongs, though the origin of the ghost, if such it was, doubtless stretches well back in time before the 1939–45 conflagration.

A correspondent, Mrs Sonia Marsh of London, wrote to me describing an uncomfortable experience she had had in the building during the 1940s, when she worked there as a clerk. It was, said Mrs Marsh, both grubby and dowdy then, a fate only to be expected for any building in central London which had seen the blitzkriegs and survived them.

Mrs Marsh, like all single women without family commitments at the time, was subject to the national requirement of long hours of service in poor conditions. In her case, this involved working over fifty hours each week, including Saturday afternoons. Eventually the staff devised a way to make the régime more reasonable by arriving fifteen minutes earlier each day, putting in an extra thirty minutes in the afternoon or appropriately cutting short the lunch

hour. In this way they occasionally rescued the precious Saturday afternoon from its workaday dustbin and enjoyed a recuperative weekend.

Unfortunately, the scheme sometimes failed to work, as on the occasion when the young Sonia, having fallen a willing victim to a series of social engagements during the week, found herself bound to work the loathed Saturday afternoon shift.

The afternoon was not prepossessing — a dank and rapidly darkening late autumn day at the end of October or early November — and her luckier, or more self-disciplined, colleagues had already left the building for their weekend destinations. Sonia was quite alone on the first floor, working somewhat resentfully in the large echoing space of what had once been the ballroom of this royal house. Within her line of vision were its twin fireplaces with blank spaces above, which had once contained valuable paintings, various elegant columns and noble windows, now wearing an unsuitable piratical air behind their blackout screens. Underfoot were bare, unlovely floors which had once, perhaps, been polished parquet. Metal filing cabinets clustered incongruously, like off-duty guardsmen, and desks, telephones and other office impedimenta did their best to obliterate the fact that the room had in its heyday been handsome and happy with music.

One little island of activity still generated energy: Sonia's small patch of light with its desk and typewriter.

The girl concentrated on her work, on the principle that the dragging time might thus pass the more quickly. However, there was an unlooked for interruption of this concentration; nothing tangible, merely a sudden strong sense of 'presence', of not being alone in the great room. For a minute she stared at the papers in front of her, then cautiously raised her head. *Imagination.* It must have been imagination. Yet no matter what her common sense told her, Sonia had a strong, and growing impression that in the dark recesses of the room, someone was lurking.

Then she turned and saw the lurker: 'a sort of greyish, swirling, triangular, smoky mass, oddly without *feet* — bobbing, receding and advancing alternately. I didn't', said Sonia Marsh in her letter to me, 'go much on it. In fact, I was *petrified.*'

She leapt to her feet, banging her shin painfully on the open drawer of a filing cabinet, and grabbed her coat ready for flight. In the middle of her panic she somehow remembered to draw the curtains to comply with blackout needs, thereby immediately darkening the terrifying scene still further. Then she raced out of the door, down the stairs and into the outer courtyard, where she finally struggled into her coat. Now she remembered sounds she had heard earlier in the afternoon, of doors opening and closing outside the ballroom. Although she had several times checked to see who else beside herself was working late that Saturday, this had

opposite
Arthur, Duke of Connaught, whose ghost is thought to haunt the ballroom at Clarence House.

55

been fruitless, and she had finally told herself that the caretaker was responsible for the noises. She left the building behind her at speed, very anxious to reach home.

On her return to work the following Monday, Sonia recounted her story to her colleagues. There was much amazement and curiosity. They seemed particularly intrigued by what had occurred, questioning her thoroughly. When she described what she had seen, one remarked: 'It was probably the old Duke of Connaught.' However, the allusion was lost on Sonia, for she had never heard of the Duke. (She had spent her formative years outside Britain, living in Soviet Russia for the decade between 1931 and 1941, and had only returned to England when she was sixteen-and-a-half.) At the time of her Clarence House encounter, the girl was between eighteen and nineteen years old.

This clearly observed and detailed description relates to a particularly alarming type of haunting — alarming, that is, for the percipient because of its formlessness and unlikeness to any identifiable human or animal shape. We are not accustomed to seeing swirling, triangular, smoky blobs of whatever substance, particularly when they waiver to and fro; and more especially when they are without feet! However, such phenomena are not unknown, and the present writer has encountered several of them. Not personally, thank goodness, but at second-hand. If I came within eyeshot of any such shifting, oscillating mist, with or without its feet, I should probably take the next plane to China.

Yet misty apparitions seem to be a valid type of haunting, and may represent an attempt to materialize by a form which has insufficient energy at its command to do more than achieve an amorphous 'blob'. Often such primitive materializations appear as a simple ball of light: I know of one which rolled along a floor and travelled up a wall and on to a mantelpiece; where, after something of a struggle, it turned into a particularly ferocious human face. Another better known example is the 'blue column' seen in the Tower of London in October 1817, when it appeared to the Keeper of the Crown Jewels, Edmund Lenthal Swifte and his family. What the Swiftes perceived was 'a cylindrical figure', filled with dense fluid. All accounts say that it hovered in the air. From this, it would seem that not only was it footless, but it was without any human shape whatever. Nonetheless, it possessed energy, for it appeared, travelled around the room and then disappeared.

The early stages of a haunting are often foggy in aspect, and appear gradually to solidify into whatever form they are going to occupy — such form, one supposes, being a representation of the original physical shape during life. But energy in varying degrees is necessary to develop it from a mere amorphous (and usually colourless) mass to the eventual maximum achievement of a seemingly-solid and fully-coloured representation. Many such 'ghosts' appear so three-dimensional as to pass for living beings. Colour, in fact, requires energy for its reproduction, just as do shape and solidity. Insufficient energy present will result in lack of colour; a circumstance which would account for the many sightings of white, grey or black spectres.

In the case of Mrs Marsh's strange apparition the energy available seems to have dwindled before even shape could be achieved.

Perhaps some legend of haunting already existed regarding Clarence House. Sonia Marsh's colleague's reaction, 'Probably the old Duke of Connaught', suggests that something of a paranormal nature had previously occurred which was known and attributed to Queen Victoria's son, Arthur, Duke of Connaught. Why this record of Connaught — if it were indeed he — should remain in the building, is impossible to say without further information. The sound of doors opening and closing in the vicinity suggests that whatever the original event causing the haunting might have been, it centred on the ballroom itself.

A strange, intriguing event, and one for which there is at present no explanation. One wonders if any of the regular inhabitants of Clarence House ever encountered the waivering mist during their residence there. It is unlikely we shall be told.

View of Clarence House with inset portraits of the Duke and Duchess of Connaught.

Cortachy Castle, Angus,
the family home of the
Earls of Airlie. The legend
persists of a phantom
drummer-boy.

CORTACHY CASTLE

Angus

Cortachy Castle in Angus, Scotland, is a home whose connection
with royalty is merely coincidental. It cannot truly be classed as a
royal home and earns inclusion here only on account of its
remarkable ghost story and the fact that one of the sons of its
ancient owning family is married to a royal princess.

Cortachy has been in the possession of the Earls of Airlie, leaders
of the Ogilvy clan, since 1625. The Ogilvys supported Charles I
against the Covenanters during the Civil War, and fought under his
heroic general, Montrose, through the 'year of miracles', 1645, when
the King's cause prospered in Scotland.

To this family belongs Princess Alexandra's husband, Mr Angus Ogilvy, younger brother of the Earl of Airlie; and the phantom drummer was a part of his childhood inheritance. On their engagement the couple attended a ball for family employees held at Cortachy, where the Princess not only met several of the Ogilvy retainers but was also apparently told the famous ghost story.

As is the way with some legends, there is more than one version of the story of the phantom drumheer of Cortachy. Marc Alexander gives it as that of a young drummer boy belonging to Clan Campbell, at the time feuding with the Ogilvys, who was taken prisoner and held at Airlie Castle. The lad was said to have died when the castle burned down in the seventeenth century and afterwards his vengeful spirit followed the family to their new home, Cortachy.

The second variation is that the boy was a drummer-herald from Clan Lindsay — also on feuding terms with the Ogilvys; the Highlanders were a remarkably quarrelsome lot — who so infuriated the Earl of Airlie by announcing himself with a defiant drumroll and then compounding the offence with an arrogant message, that the Earl had him seized and flung from the castle battlements.

The third and most romantic tale is also the one most widely believed. The drummer in this account was one of the Earl's own servants, and having fallen in love with the then Countess of Airlie, proceeded to have an affair with her. When the fact was discovered, the Earl, a resentful and far from complaisant husband, had the presumptuous young man fastened into his own drum which was then forcibly propelled out of a high turret window. The youth survived this uncomfortable method of execution just long enough to curse the Earl to his face, promising that his ghost should haunt the Ogilvy family as long as the castle was in their possession.

One further variant of the legend arises from the last. It is that the Earl's lady was not the mistress of the young drummer but his sister, she not daring to reveal his identity since he was at the time an outlaw. This seems a spuriously clumsy version of the tale and does not appear to be widely accepted.

Whichever of the accounts is true, what is irrefutable is the drummer's fulfilment of his dying curse. From time to time through the intervening centuries, the sound of drumming has been heard in and around Cortachy Castle. However, the drum-playing is not random but purposeful; it occurs only before the death of a member of the family, and as such falls into the familiar pattern of a warning haunting.

Elliott O'Donnell, a keen ghosthunter of the nineteen-forties and fifties, records an account (also noted by Alexander) of a Miss Dalrymple, who accompanied by her maid, Mrs Ann Day, stayed at Cortachy Castle in 1845. While she was dressing for dinner on the first evening of her visit, she was surprised to hear the distinct and rhythmic beating of a drum somewhere beneath her window. Her maid was not present in the room at the time, and although questioned on her return, said that she had heard nothing which resembled drumming.

Miss Dalrymple forgot about the sound, for it seemed of little importance, and it was not until the company were half way through dinner that she casually asked her host who his drummer was. Lord Airlie turned pale, Lady Airlie appeared upset and Miss Dalrymple realized she had made a social gaffe of some kind, though she had no idea why her remark should have had such a surprising effect. Later, when the party had re-assembled in the drawing-room, she asked a member of the family about the incident, and was met with: 'What, have you never heard of the drummer boy?' Miss Dalrymple, puzzled, replied that she had not, and asked who in the world he might be. 'Why,' said her informant, 'he goes about the house playing his drum whenever there is a death impending in the family.' He had, it seemed, been heard shortly before the death of the previous Countess, the Earl's former wife, and this fact had accounted for the Earl's sudden pallor and his wife's distress. The drummer, Miss Dalrymple was assured, was a very unpleasant subject to the Ogilvys.

The matter might have been allowed to remain there if the drummer had only rested on his laurels. However, the next morning at breakfast when presumably hosts and guests were peacefully salting their porridge, Miss Dalrymple's maid heard the clear, penetrating rataplan of a drum, being energetically beaten somewhere outside in the courtyard. It did not stay there. From the courtyard it moved into the house, echoing and re-echoing and growing gradually louder as it approached the turret in which Miss Dalrymple and her maid were lodged. The following morning Mrs Day's experience was exactly repeated for her mistress's benefit, at which point Miss Dalrymple decided to end her visit. The rat-a-tat-tat of the invisible drummer would probably have been discounted by both women once they had left the Castle, had not the Earl's second Countess also died about five or six months after the event, reportedly leaving a note in her desk declaring that she had known the drumming had been for her.

A delay of so long in the fulfilment of a prophecy (or a curse, depending on how one looks at it) seems to suggest coincidence rather than parapsychology, yet had the Countess actually believed at the time that the prophesied death would be hers, then her mind's own suggestibility might have brought about that very event. The efficacy of hypnosis, both other– and self-induced, suggests that such things are possible, for our minds appear to have a powerful and unguessed at influence upon the way our bodies behave. Primitive tribes have known very well how to bring about a death without lifting a finger against their victim. They merely inform the selected person that he is going to die, and his own fear and faith in the intention appear to do the rest. If humans possess a will to live which can occasionally overcome death, they can also sometimes exhibit a will to die which will effectively extinguish life.

As a corollary to the Dalrymple experience, Elliott O'Donnell himself had an unusual encounter while staying not far from Cortachy. In his hotel was an elderly visitor named Porter, who had in boyhood often visited relatives living near Cortachy Castle. He had struck up a friendship with a local boy named Alec, and on one occasion the two lads decided to spend part of one night rabbiting in a spinney adjoining the Earl of Airlie's estate. They planned their entrance with care, for Alec had once or twice been caught by the estate's keepers and threatened with proceedings for trespass.

To get into the spinney the boys had to climb a granite wall and drop over into the pitch darkness of the wood. The fact that mantraps were often set there by the gamekeepers made the expedition both more alarming and more adventurous. However, they gained access and having found the main warren under the wood's tallest trees, they set their ferrets to work. Young Porter and Alec had accounted for three rabbits and were feeling pleased with themselves, when a strong and inexplicable sense of physical coldness began to creep over them. Looking up, they were astonished to see the figure of a very tall keeper standing close by them. Neither lad uttered a sound, and indeed each was for the moment incapable either of speech or movement. All they could clearly see was the tall, slight shape of a man with 'a gleaming white face, and a round glittering something that puzzled us both exceedingly'. Then to Porter occurred the idea that what he was seeing might just not be a keeper but something very different. And at that moment the figure turned and began to move towards the boys. In a frenzy of terror they turned and fled back to the wall, with the sound of the figure's footsteps hard on their heels. But worse than this was another sound which followed them: the unmistakable ran-a-tan-tan of a muffled drum.

Over the wall, falling and stumbling, they went, but the footsteps seemed to die away in the direction of the castle. The drumbeats, too, gradually faded into the distance and were finally silenced. A few days later one of the Airlie family died, and the boys for the first time learned the legend of the phantom drummer.

Some months later O'Donnell returned to the same hotel and was distressed to learn that his old acquaintance, Porter, had himself died. Perhaps it was this fact, or merely the ghosthunter's curiosity which prompted him. He decided to try to replicate Porter's own boyhood adventure, and at once set off in the bright moonlight to find the glade in the spinney of which the older man had told him.

61

KETTLE-DRUMS.

O'Donnell reached it with no more trouble than a few bramble scratches, a bump on the head and several tears to his clothing.

But once in the glade, something strange occurred. A slight breeze in the pine-tops gradually grew until it reverberated, sounding just a little like a tattoo played on an invisible drum. O'Donnell turned to go. And immediately saw what he had come — and dreaded — to see: a tall thin figure with a dead white face, its head topped by something small, round, glittering. It remained momentarily still, then glided from the path and vanished into the shadows. A breeze followed its going; and a long reverberation moaned through the trees; rat-tat-tat, rat-tat-tat. O'Donnell's feet winged him back to his hotel.

What did he see, if anything? We shall never know now, but it is possible that the combination of a smart crack on the head as he fell from the wall into the spinney (it had knocked him unconscious for a few minutes), plus a sharply heightened sensitivity on account of his expectations, may have predisposed him to see and hear the phantom drummer. In other words, the experience may have been totally subjective and a temporary creation of Mr O'Donnell's own mind.

On the other hand, he may just have encountered the actual presence of the ghostly drummer of Cortachy Castle!

One further curious point remains from this series of strange episodes. What was the 'round glittering something' which Porter and Alec had seen, and the something small, round and glittering which O'Donnell perceived many years later; both objects seemingly connected with the head of the apparition?

There are two possibilities: either they represented a cap or military headdress worn by the figure during its lifetime; or represented, perhaps, the drum. Not, then, a great drum to entomb a youth's body, but a small thing of the kettledrum type, jammed over a man's face and head before his body was flung from the castle battlements. A macabre and unexpected touch to a weird tale. Ghosts, if one pays enough attention to them, often tell us as much about the facts of their original lives and deaths as they do about their times.

Dalkeith House, near Edinburgh, which was constructed in its present form between 1700 and 1715, although parts of the building date back to the twelfth century. Although it is not known whether the building is haunted, a dog's hair stands on end whenever it passes a certain spot in the house.

DALKEITH HOUSE

nr. Edinburgh

Dalkeith House is another of the several strongholds of the powerful Douglas clan, and like many of Scotland's fortified houses, has changed hands a number of times during the course of its chequered history. It was occupied during part of the sixteenth century by James Douglas, Earl of Morton, Regent during the infancy of James VI and I. He was a tough, vigorous man in the true fashion of the Douglases, and during his regency Dalkeith House became known as 'the Lion's Den', a self-explanatory title.

The staircase at Dalkeith House. During the reign of James IV the Royal court transferred from Edinburgh to Dalkeith to escape the plague.

The Buccleuchs bought the house and lands in the mid-seventeenth century, and during this turbulent period civil war raged in both England and Scotland, though some lessening of tension occurred during the period of the Commonwealth. Peace gave both Scots and English time to reflect on the kind of government they wished to have and the way of life which would offer them most in terms of quality.

General George Monck had become Governor of Scotland under Cromwell's régime, and chose Dalkeith House as his headquarters. According to the interesting *Memoirs* of Princess Alice, Duchess of Gloucester, the General planned Charles II's restoration from this particular home of her ancestors. Once Charles Stuart came to the

James Scott, Duke of Monmouth, 1st Duke of Buccleuch, c.1683 (portrait after William Wissing).

throne, he was happy to marry his illegitimate eldest son, James, Duke of Monmouth, to the Countess Anna Buccleuch. Monmouth then took the title of Duke of Buccleuch and three years later the title of Duchess was conferred on Anna in order to preserve title and lands when Monmouth was disgraced and executed for treason during the reign of his uncle, James II.

Princess Alice remarks that some dark happening in the house's past might have accounted for 'the spooky spot' which existed between double doors near an upstairs drawing-room. The young Lady Alice and her sister, Sybil, had to pass this dreaded area *en route* for their mother's drawing-room and always, as they approached it, the children linked hands, shut their eyes and shot past as fast as their legs would carry them. Many years afterwards Princess Alice chanced to mention this childhood experience to an uncle, and was told that he, too, had had the same sensation at the exact spot she described.

Nowadays Dalkeith House (local people still refer to it as a 'Palace' on account of its having been used by James IV of Scotland as a refuge from the plague) is a study centre for Wisconsin University and is furnished, not with the old and beautiful pieces belonging to the Buccleuchs, but with comfortable functional items suitable for its present usage. The shell of the building remains the same, of course; panelling, noble windows, handsome ceilings and staircase remind of the house's distinguished history.

Another link with the past appears to have stayed in place, too. One of the house's present official inhabitants informs me that there is 'a spooky room' (her words) off an apartment in which Queen Victoria slept on her frequent visits to Dalkeith. My correspondent's dog, when accompanying its owner into the room invariably 'freezes on the spot, (and) her hair stands on end'. It seems that at this juncture the heavy double doors invariably slam shut and the humans, at least, find themselves tiptoeing out, as though afraid to disturb the room's occupant. Spooky, indeed, and so similar to the account given by Princess Alice that the two descriptions would seem to relate to the one area.

A further remark by my informant suggests that, during the tenancy of the last official body, noises were heard from this 'double-door' area at night which suggested a paranormal origin. It will be interesting to see if they recur when the next tenants take over.

Beyond this very mild and not unfriendly haunting — if that is what it is — Dalkeith House seems a most pleasant and civilized place in which to be, with its magnificent wooded surroundings and its lofty perch on the banks of the River North Esk. Most august bodies would surely find its influence on their conference deliberations entirely beneficial.

DRUMLANRIG CASTLE

Dumfriesshire

The North front and entrance of Drumlanrig Castle, Dumfriesshire, owned by the Duke of Buccleuch, which dates from the seventeenth century. One of its rooms is haunted by a giant monkey or ape once kept as a pet.

When Princess Alice, the Dowager Duchess of Gloucester, was a child, one of her life's delights was the annual visit paid by her family to Drumlanrig Castle in Dumfriesshire, the home of her grandparents. The attraction of Drumlanrig for the little Lady Alice Montagu-Douglas-Scott was its beauty, and it is indeed a delectable small castle of the seventeenth century, originally built by William Douglas, the first Duke of Queenberry. Castles like Drumlanrig, half palatial home and half serious fortress, began to appear in Scotland when the union with England was consolidated, and once the last hope of the Clans — the Jacobite cause — came to its bloody ending.

So Drumlanrig kept the atmosphere of defensiveness from which the Scots had not yet freed themselves after their violent Middle Ages, yet reached out to the serene beauty of its native countryside which the new unity with England safeguarded. Princess Alice, in her delightful *Memoirs*, describes the grassy park, tree enshaded, which ran down to the river Nith, and the banked gardens with their gravel paths and immaculate box hedges. Woodland backed

opposite
Drumlanrig Castle as seen from the grounds.

69

Another view of
Drumlanrig Castle, built
of pink granite.

the view and the open moorland lay beyond that. But it was the castle itself which dominated then as it does now, its pink granite walls glittering with mica in the sunlight.

There was a darker side for the children who visited it, for on autumn nights the equinoctial gales howled around the castle's four turrets, and those who lay awake were left to conjure up whatever they knew of the building's history and to imagine what ghosts its story might have provided for such a night as this.

In fact Princess Alice's mother and the latter's sister had seen Drumlanrig's main ghost on their very first visit to the house. They were young girls then and both single and beautiful. Their way to bed lay along one of the castle's many long, draughty passageways, and the flame of their candle threw back alarming shadows as they drew near their bedroom. Before they even reached its door, however, they saw what seemed to be some furry creature moving towards them down the corridor. And at that moment their frail candle blew out, leaving them in absolute darkness. Not surprisingly, the girls were frightened speechless and bolting for their bedroom door, flung it open and fell inside. Although presumably they mentioned the event to someone of the household the following day, there seems to have been no further discussion afterwards or any follow-up of the incident. Perhaps the girls convinced

previous page
A romantic view of
Drumlanrig Castle from a
nineteenth-century
engraving.

72

The Front Hall. The
entrance hall contains,
among other treasures, a
section of tapestry
needlework by Mary,
Queen of Scots, and a
copper kettle in which
Lord Soulis was boiled
alive at Hermitage Castle.

themselves that they had imagined the furry animal; or perhaps some feeling of superstitious fear forbade any talk of the thing again.

One of the sisters, however, was to encounter it a second time several years later, when she had married the son of the Buccleuch family and become the Countess of Dalkeith, the future mother of Princess Alice. There were guests in the house at the time, and one of them, Lady Mabel Howard, happened to discover the Countess standing stock-still in the hall, looking decidedly shaken and white. On being asked what ailed her, she replied that she had just seen a huge monkey sitting on one of the chairs. The astonished Lady Mabel assumed her hostess to be suffering at the very least from indigestion, but the Countess was adamant. Not indigestion but the sight of the giant monkey was the cause of her pallor. She could not explain what she saw, and may not even have remembered the earlier experience with her sister.

The ghost cropped up again during the First World War when the castle, in common with many other large houses, was turned into a hospital for the wounded. It had, as was usual at the time, an appointed matron and a complement of nurses, though the local organizer responsible for the smooth running of things seems to have been, in Drumlanrig's case, the wife of the Buccleuch's agent.

73

The matron does not appear to have spent long in her post, for one morning she asked to see the agent's wife as a matter of urgency. If this suggested to the organizer that the administration was not meeting professional requirements, she was soon disillusioned. The matron announced without ceremony that she could not stay in her post, but intended to leave at once. The foolish woman, even when pressed for reasons, refused to be specific, merely saying that she had 'seen something awful in the night,' and must leave. Her continued refusal to give further information she qualified by saying that she feared 'the family' would not like her to do so. Noble families were regarded with a great deal more awe seventy years ago than they are today. However, leave she did, and no one discovered why. Until, that is, the end of the war. It was then that some person, presumably connected with the castle either by ties of family or service, was examining books and documents in the muniments room and came across an inventory for the building dated 1700. The room which the distraught matron had used was listed simply as: 'Yellow Monkey or Haunted Room'.

Now if as early as 1700 the room was known to be haunted, then the origin of the haunting must have pre-dated the entry by (possibly) a considerable time. One does not usually call a room haunted on the evidence of a single experience, and it therefore seems likely that the yellow monkey — almost certainly the 'furry thing' seen by the two sisters, and the 'huge monkey' referred to by the Countess a few years later — once lived in the flesh in Drumlanrig Castle. Maybe it was brought back from tropical travels by one of the family; or purchased from some menagerie as a novelty. Animals were not regarded then as they are today, but were often thought of as prestige symbols or exotic curiosities. Perhaps the monkey was kept in the castle as a pet — though its size in spectral form suggests it was more likely an ape than a monkey — and allowed to roam about the house at will. Whatever its original purpose in being where it was later seen, its presence must have registered very strongly in the area to survive for so long a time; at least two hundred and fifteen years, probably more. How, one wonders, did it die to cause such a vivid record to remain? Perhaps somewhere in the muniments of this present Buccleuch Castle there are other references to the strange beast.

Princess Alice does relate another incident in Drumlanrig in which she herself was involved. She had contracted diphtheria, and since it was before the days of inoculations against the disease, she was seriously ill and possibly delirious, though this last fact is by no means certain and after so long an interval cannot be attested to one way or the other. It seems that the young invalid saw a small girl, wearing a long dress, appear at her bedside, the unusual factor being that the apparition's feet were three or four inches from the floor. The Princess speculates that 'she' may well have belonged to the castle's earlier history, and a time when the floor level was considerably higher than it had been at the time of her illness. Had the girl, asks the Princess, actually once lived in that very room, generations before? Or was 'she', after all, a product of the diphtheria delirium? If any other witnesses of this apparition exist, their evidence could possibly clarify the matter.

Princess Alice, an intelligently open-minded lady, also had a slight experience at another of her family homes (see Dalkeith House). And a third Buccleuch property (see Newark Castle), though long since ruined and disused, afforded the present author an uneasy half hour several years ago.

Antony Hippisley-Cox, in his useful gazeteer, *Haunted Britain*, cites yet another ghost at Drumlanrig, that of a Lady Anne Douglas, whom he states walks there with her head in her hand. I can find no other reference to this haunting, nor to the Lady Anne Douglas referred to. Princess Alice mentions the Countess Anna Buccleuch who was given in marriage to Charles II's bastard son by Lucy Walters, James Duke of Monmouth; and other sources refer to this particular lady as the Lady Anne Scott: which merely confounds confusion. However, this Lady Anne was not, I think, executed, though her husband, Monmouth, certainly was for his rebellion against his uncle, James II, in an ill-advised attempt to seize the throne.

C. LYCAON. L.

London Published by G.B. Whittaker

GATCOMBE PARK

Gloucestershire

Any sightseer looking for Gatcombe Park from the road is on a sticky wicket. Gatcombe, like Highgrove for the Prince of Wales and Nether Lypiatt for Prince Michael of Kent, is the name of an estate rather than a village, and Princess Anne and Captain Mark Phillips are protected from casual inspection by a long drive, several rolling hills and sundry well-placed belts of trees; not to mention the usual very necessary security precautions.

The day I passed by, a police sergeant was on duty outside the nearest gate, waiting for an obviously VIP car to emerge. Also waiting was an equally transparent security limousine. We stopped to ask directions to a village some five miles distant and were courteously given them; then asked to move clear of the drive entrance. My companion and I thought it as ill-mannered to linger as to obstruct and drove away. I had already discovered that no one in the neighbourhood had heard of the Gatcombe ghost.

I suspect there is not much of a ghost there. It is said to be the spectre of a black dog, which supposedly haunts the grounds.

Now black dogs are by no means scarce in England and Wales — or for all I know, Scotland, either. In fact, they are as common as gnats on summer evenings, rain on Bank Holidays and ground elder in my garden.

There are several odd elements in black dog legends. For one thing, most of the creatures have names. In Norfolk and Suffolk, the animal is known as Black Shuck. In Lancashire it is named the padfoot, while in other areas the term barguest or trash is used.

The terms of the dog's visitation are usually similar, irrespective of its particular county. Invariably the report is of seeing a huge black animal resembling a dog, but with large glaring eyes (or some say glowing eyes). Its appearance is commonly supposed to presage ill-luck, sometimes to the point of tragedy.

I know of one case where the creature was encountered along a country road in Cambridgeshire, where it leaped over the bonnet of a car travelling towards the Iron Age camp a few miles from the city. 'A huge black animal, bigger than any dog we'd ever seen,' said the car's owners. It vanished into allotments on the far side of the road, and although the motorists searched for half an hour, they did not find any living dog.

Another car-driver in Suffolk was followed along a woodside by a giant black dog of an Alsatian type which, no matter how fast he travelled, not only had no trouble in keeping pace but actually gained on the vehicle. A thoroughly alarmed motorist was only relieved from the animal's presence — and its fixed stare at him — when he pulled clear of the wood. It then disappeared as abruptly as it had arrived. It transpired that the wood was named Wolf Wood; a fact which may be significant in determining the nature of Black Shuck and the rest of his mythic kin.

For the ghostly black dogs are, I believe, mythical in origin; or, to alter the perspective slightly, are possibly derived from racial memories of the Celtic religion. The Celts, among other animals revered and worshipped wolves, and the wolf cult may have included the keeping of sacred animals. Yet the wolf cult itself seems to have been an aspect of fertility-worship, the wolf (or dog) being regarded as the sacred corn spirit, to be killed at the end of harvest to ensure the following year's fertility.

Andrew Mackenzie in *Apparitions and Ghosts* recalls that most ghostly dogs are said to be black in hue, though occasionally other colours are mentioned. In Little Cawthorpe, Lincolnshire, for instance, a large white dog is said to haunt. Theo Brown, a member of the Society for Psychical Research and author of a paper on dog apparitions, noticed that most of the black dog reports come from Lincolnshire and Devonshire, and that the Lincolnshire variety are often not so much sinister as protective, though only towards women and only those of their own county. Next time I visit my native countryside I may well try out this theory.

overleaf
An aerial view of Gatcombe Park, Gloucestershire, the home of Princess Anne and Captain Mark Phillips. Legend has it that its grounds are haunted by a black dog or wolf.

From all of which it would seem that black dog hauntings are rural in origin, extremely ancient and probably derived from fertility cults, possibly being handed down even from Neolithic times.

Gatcombe Park, peaceful and untroubled now in its bowl of green-grey hills, may once have known the worship of the corn-spirit in the form of either wolf or black dog. And somewhere, hazy in the unconscious of the local people a memory may still linger, surfacing rarely but effectively as the story of a ghost. We all carry certain ancestral memories, unremembered and quite unrecognized. They lie about the twentieth century in the form of superstitions, pseudo-hauntings and bits of occult lumber.

Gatcombe, with its nearness to the infinitely old Neolithic religious centres of the south-west, seems to hold one hazy and fast-fading imprint of its childhood. It has, I think, no ghosts.

GLAMIS CASTLE

Angus

> All hail, Macbeth! hail to thee,
>   Thane of Glamis!
> All hail, Macbeth! hail to thee,
>   Thane of Cawdor!
> All hail, Macbeth! that shalt be king hereafter!

Thus the witches to Macbeth, confirming his title, castle, lands and promising the royal vista which lay beyond; tantalizingly beyond.

In 1372 the thanage of Glamis was granted to Sir John Lyon by King Robert II, and four years later the Thane married the King's daughter, Princess Joanna. There have been royal connections at Glamis ever since.

However, the place was not originally intended as a stronghold, but was meant as a hunting lodge for the monarch, in an area then still heavily wooded by the ancient forest of Scotland. It was Shakespeare who bestowed on Macbeth the title of Thane of Glamis, using a playwright's artistic licence, for Glamis was not a thanage in the eleventh century. By the time John Lyon married his princess, Robert II had changed Glamis from a thanage to a feudal barony.

King Malcolm II, some say mortally wounded in battle, others that he was murdered in Glamis, died there in 1034 and a room in the building still bears his name. His grandson and heir, Duncan I, was killed, probably near Elgin by his cousin, Macbeth, who then succeeded to the crown. Shakespeare took the various bloodthirsty events — fairly commonplace occurrences in early Scottish politics — and spun them into a magnificent tragedy; but the history is seen through his dramatic vision and is not necessarily exactly as it occurred.

Glamis Castle through the ages has attracted to itself a wealth of legend and lore. The earliest story concerns its siting, for it is said that the building was begun on Hunter's Hill nearby, but each night the work of the previous day was pulled down by the fairies, until eventually the workmen took the hint and moved the building to the low-lying plain of Strathmore, near Dundee.

Whatever the reason for the choice of site, the castle eventually raised has an extraordinary quality of beauty and majesty, almost of other-worldliness. With its castellations and close-bunched, many-capped turrets, the mellow red sandstone building gives an impression of formidable strength, power and concentrated history. And the snow-tipped, distant Grampians lend permanence to a scene whose very beauty otherwise suggests the opposite.

overleaf
Glamis Castle, Scotland, famous, among other legends, for its 'concealed room'.

Much of Sir John Lyon's original structure still remains, incorporated into later adaptations. This Sir John, known as 'The White Lyon' on account of his light hair and complexion, was murdered in his bed by Sir James Lindsay of Crawford, Scotland's Ambassador to England, with whose family the Lyons had sustained a long blood feud. His successor, another John, renewed the connection with the Royal Family by marrying Robert II's great-granddaughter, and during their tenure, further castle-improvement took place.

However, although with this close royal involvement the Lyon family seemed secure in its position, its safety was to be badly shaken two centuries later, following the death of John, 6th Lord Glamis. This John had been unwise enough to marry a daughter of the Douglas clan, the beautiful and virtuous Janet Douglas. Unfortunately the ruling monarch, James V, when young, had suffered from a dominating stepfather — also a Douglas — and from indignities and humiliations at the hands of other members of that clan. James, with the Tudor blood in his veins of his mother Margaret, Henry VIII's sister, had a strong vindictive streak in his make-up, as well as a quixotic quality and a curiosity about life outside palace walls. Unfortunately, for Janet, Lady Glamis, twice widowed and therefore politically as well as personally vulnerable, King James's hatred of her clan had reached the level of paranoia. He seized her castle, her person and that of her young son, accusing her of witchcraft — an obviously trumped-up charge — and had her condemned to death. During Lady Glamis's long imprisonment, the King and his Queen, Mary of Guise, moved into Glamis Castle and lived there for five years, ransacking the place of all its treasures and leaving little for the young heir to inherit.

Young Lord Glamis, however, remained in prison, sentenced like his mother to die, and only saved when the King predeceased him. Janet, his well-loved and popular mother, went to the stake, convicted on the false charges of witchcraft and planning to poison James V. She was burnt 'with great commiseration of the people, being in the prime of her years, of a singular beauty, and suffering all, though a woman, with a manlike courage'.

It is this unfortunate lady whose ghost is said to have been occasionally seen, floating above the castle clock-tower and surrounded by a lurid glow, an appearance which may represent the appalling manner of her death.

A later Lord, the 9th Earl, Patrick, was responsible for extensive renovations and improvements to a castle which had begun to fall into disrepair, and much of the fine interior of the building is due to this Lord Glamis. It was he who re-modelled the stair turret and tower in 1606. In the older parts of the castle there are walls fifteen feet thick and in some of these secret staircases and closets were built, two having been discovered in comparatively recent times.

Secret rooms, also, were a common occurrence in the older Scottish castles, designed originally as a refuge for the family in time of danger, though probably used for other purposes when occasion demanded.

Glamis's most famous concealed room is one of the few which remain hidden. Its whereabouts is by tradition known to only three persons at any one time — the current Earl, his eldest son and one other, who is trusted by them. This rigorous requirement is apparently never breached, and whatever the nature of the room itself, it seems to be associated with some grim family secret.

Various guesses have been made as to its nature, and it is not surprising that legends attached to the castle's history have been evoked. One is that of a fifteenth-century Lord of Glamis, who fell to gambling with Lord Crawford, a bearded giant known as 'Earl Beardie' or the 'Tiger Earl', the pair playing cards in the hidden room on the eve of the Sabbath. So engrossed were they, that even when warned by a servant of the rapid approach of Sunday they refused to quit their game, and both swore that they would play the game out though it took until Doomsday. Whereupon midnight struck, and a stranger appeared in the room. True to diabolic tradition he informed them that they would be held to their pact.

'Earl Beardie' is reported to have appeared a number of times, once to a daughter of Lord Castletown, and on several occasions to children, who woke up screaming that a huge, bearded man had leaned over their beds and looked at them. Others have awakened to find that the surrounding furnishings have transformed themselves from modern to ancient at the moment of the ghost's appearance and reverted as soon as he vanished. These rooms are no longer in use, according to Peter Underwood's report, though this does not prevent sounds of movement coming from within them.

There is also a fearful story arising from an old feud between the Ogilvys and Lindsays. After a clan battle, a number of defeated Ogilvys arrived outside Glamis asking for protection. The then Earl, in an understandable desire not to offend either antagonist, admitted the fugitives and put them in a remote room, assuring them of safety. He then locked the door and left them. Whether he actually forgot their presence, or whether the neglect was intentional, he did not return, and the little band died of starvation.

They remained in their remote tomb until a Victorian Lord Strathmore unlocked the room door — and fainted. He is said to have beheld a room full of skeletons.

From time to time the sound of banging and thunderous knocking has been heard in this area of the castle, and although it has on occasion been attributed to the noise made by the erection of the martyred Lady Janet's scaffold, it is unlikely to be so since her death took place in distant Edinburgh. The desperate Ogilvys, on the other hand, were imprisoned in Glamis and left to die. One imagines they would not have accepted this fate without forceful protest.

Other stories designed to make flesh creep and hair stand aloft are the tall spectre known as 'Jack the Runner'; and the figure of a small Negro page, thought to have been cruelly treated during his lifetime, who appears outside the door of the present Queen Mother's sitting-room; and the frightened face of a young woman seen at a tower window by a guest in the castle. There is a suitably gory corollary to this last, which states that afterwards the man heard a fearful scream, followed minutes later by the sight of an old woman crossing the courtyard beneath him with a heavy bundle thrown across her shoulder, leaving the guest convinced that it contained the body of the girl whose face he had briefly glimpsed.

This, of course, is the sort of tale which makes the unbeliever in parapsychology cry 'What utter rubbish!' and switch on the television to watch snooker as an antidote. However, there is a peculiar sequel. The man who had been Glamis's guest, years later found himself caught in a snowstorm in Italy, and took shelter in a nearby monastery. While there the monks told him of a woman living in a neighbouring convent, whose tongue had been cut out and hands amputated to prevent her revealing some fearful family secret she had discovered. The guest, without apparently any foundation for his surmise, believed her to be the girl he had seen at Glamis.

This story is unsatisfactory in every way, for it contains neither names, dates nor reliable evidence. The only justification for quoting it is that it is so well known that one suspects it may have its roots in distant fact.

A much more solid tale is that of the so-called monster of Glamis; although 'monster' is a term belonging strictly to earlier, less-enlightened days, if the individual so described was, as I suspect, merely a physically (and possibly mentally) handicapped child.

According to legend, this child was a first-born son who should have inherited title, castle and lands, but because of the hideousness of his malformation and incapacity had to be set aside in favour of a second son. He would never be fit for a normal life and responsibilities, so what should be done with him? The family is said to have taken the only course available by confining him somewhere in the castle, where he need not be seen; for since he could never be acknowledged as the heir, his presence must, of necessity, be concealed. And what better place for concealment than one of the secret rooms?

Certainly the conviction that a deformed human lived within the castle walls has persisted — fed, no doubt, by reports of occasional sightings, curious apparently paranormal experiences and what, for want of a better word, one must call dreams; though dreams of an extraordinary kind, where the dreamer found herself or himself in a bare prison-like cell, watching a barely-human creature shuffling about the room.

Such stories are all very well, and are often embroidered between one generation and the next, but what one must ask is the reason for their persistence? Was there ever, in historical fact, an eldest son who failed for some reason to inherit his patrimony? An entry in Debrett's Peerage of 1841 may supply a possible answer, as Jean Goodman's excellent *Royal Scotland* makes plain. It reads:

GEORGE LYON, Lord Glamis, b. 6 Feb. 1801, m. 21 Dec. 1820, Charlotte, da. of Charles Grinstead, esq., and d. 27 Jan. 1834, leaving issues, 1. a son b. and d. 18 Oct. 1821; 2. THOMAS GEORGE, Lord Glamis, b. 28 Sept. 1822; in the army; 3. Claude, b. 19 June 1824.

Supposing the son born on 18 October 1821 did not die within hours of his birth. If he were indeed hopelessly handicapped, how would the young couple have dealt with their cruel dilemma? Perhaps they took the only course open to them at the time, which was to rear the child away from public view, to treat him as well as they could while doing their best to cover the social 'disgrace' and scandal of what had befallen them.

One actual sighting is worth reporting because of its factual detail. A slater repairing the roof of the castle suddenly found he had unwittingly penetrated the great secret; he came down the ladder in some distress, insisting that he had seen a terrible sight. The agent to the estate took charge of him, and after consultations with the family and official advisers, the workman swore never to reveal what he had witnessed. In return for his silence, he and his family were granted a pension and a new life in Australia.

These are a few of the many legends of Glamis, and they add spice to a building of long and distinguished history and magnificent presence. Here you will find a plethora of portraits, records of family members of first the Lyons and then the Bowes-Lyons (Bowes became added to the name when the 9th Earl married the great Durham heiress, Mary Eleanor Bowes of Streatham Castle, in the eighteenth century).

Among the portraits are two thought to represent James V and his Queen, Mary of Guise, that royal couple who had occupied and pillaged the castle for several years after judicially killing the Lady of Glamis, Lady Janet. Their daughter, Mary, Queen of Scots, later stayed briefly at the castle when *en route* to quell Huntly's rebellion. She and her companions arrived at Glamis in atrocious weather from roads ankle-deep in mud. However, the Queen was in high spirits, rejoicing in this adventure, and saying that she would wish 'to lie all night in the fields, or to walk upon the Causeway with a pack, a buckler and a broadsword'.

Another view of the
exterior of Glamis Castle.

The castle boasts some fine painting. There is an exceptionally interesting portrait of Queen Elizabeth I, for it is one of the very few which shows a marked likeness to her mother, Anne Boleyn.

Much of the art work in the house is by Jakob de Wett or de Wit, a Dutch painter of the seventeenth century, and the chapel in particular contains some excellent work, in contrast to the markedly inferior canvases at Holyroodhouse by the same artist.

Perhaps the two most striking rooms are the crypt (formerly the lower hall of the fourteenth-century tower house where the servants would dine) and the drawing-room. It is the crypt which is said to hide the secret room in one of its immensely thick walls. The drawing-room is a place of palatial beauty, and has a handsome arched ceiling.

Overall, Glamis in spite of its mysteries and rumours of mysteries, has beauty and comfort and the feeling of a house long-lived in by one family. There is a sense of continuity and of small events building a long tradition. The lion, that symbol of the owning house, is ubiquitous, but the feudal pride it represents is counterbalanced by more intimate touches. Glamis, until comparatively recent times continued to employ a family jester, and his suit of striped motley, be-belled and buttoned, is still kept. (The family once also employed its own hangman!)

There are echoes, too, of the present royal connection, for when its young daughter, the Lady Elizabeth, married HRH the Duke of York in 1923, a suite was set apart for future royal use. The second child of their marriage, HRH the Princess Margaret, was actually born at Glamis, being the first royal baby in direct succession to the throne to be born in Scotland for three hundred years.

On the abdication of King Edward VIII, the Duke of York became King George VI and his Duchess Queen Consort. Their royal children are, of course, full cousins to the present Earl of Strathmore and Kinghorne, Fergus, 17th Earl, master of Glamis.

The castle, despite its exciting and often violent history, is primarily a modern (and ancient) home for a distinguished Scottish family, which has seen great celebrations as well as fierce tragedies. Like most families with this type of background, the extraordinariness of their ancestors' adventures is accepted unquestioningly, taken for granted; as are the legends of the old building they themselves inhabit. Home is home, and whether it is built of red brick, Cotswold stone or Highland sandstone, it holds the memory of its inhabitants, the register and record of their deeds and emotions over the years.

To live in Glamis is to touch most of the history of Scotland, and must be a cause for pride.

HAMPTON COURT PALACE

London

Many beautiful buildings grace the banks of the River Thames, but none is lovelier than the palace built by the butcher's son of Ipswich.

Thomas Wolsey's humble origins did not prevent him from rising to one of the most prestigious appointments in Tudor England. He became first Archbishop of York, then a cardinal and finally Lord Chancellor of England. His influence with his King, Henry VIII, was considerable, and on this account, as well as by reason of his own formidable abilities, he became the most powerful commoner in the realm.

In 1514 he acquired a tract of land on the banks of the Thames, and proceeded to build on it such a grand country house that in the general view it qualified as a palace. In the King's view, also. Henry was liable to become suspicious of over-powerful or grandiloquent subjects.

Wolsey, profitably rapacious, as were many medieval churchmen, also had a successful political career, being particularly interested in foreign policy, and from 1518 to 1529 he virtually dominated the government. Despots, however, are rarely loved, even by those they serve. Disliked by both parliament and people, Wolsey finally held on to power purely by the support of the King. When he failed to obtain an annulment of Henry's first marriage (to Catherine of Aragon), the King withdrew his goodwill, to bestow it on Thomas Cromwell who had promised what Wolsey failed to perform. Wolsey, seeing the threatening writing on the wall, tried to buy himself out of disfavour by offering Henry the palace he had so much admired, Hampton Court. It was characteristic of this particular monarch to accept the gift, while not altering his intended course a jot. He summoned Wolsey from his see of York to answer charges of treason, and the Cardinal, sick at heart as in body, set out on a journey destined, he knew, to end in the Tower and execution. He reached Leicester and could go no further. Lying on his death bed, he said ruefully: 'Had I but served God as diligently as I have served my King, He would not have given me over in my grey hairs.' At Leicester he died. Henry was already established in Hampton Court.

Henry VIII took all his Queens, apart from the first, to Wolsey's old palace, and it is hardly surprising in view of their stressful marital record that it contains psychic echoes of the period. His children also would use the place, though they were to leave behind no post-death traces.

opposite
Henry VIII c.1542 (artist unknown).

91

CARDINAL   WOLSEY

Cardinal Wolsey who
made a gift of Hampton
Court to Henry VIII.

Anne Boleyn has been seen, downcast and sad of countenance, drifting along corridors in the blue dress she wore for the portrait which still hangs in the building. There have been no sightings of this ghost in recent times at Hampton Court, however, though she is liberally recorded elsewhere.

The most spectacular haunting is certainly that by Catherine Howard, a cousin of Anne Boleyn, whom two wives later she followed into wedlock with this dangerous King.

Catherine, brought up in the country in Norfolk, had been given considerable freedom in youth. She was one of a group of young noblewomen supervised by the old Duchess of Norfolk, and the slackness of such supervision was reflected in the sexual liberty enjoyed by these girls and the aristocratic youths who also frequented the Norfolks' household. Though Catherine was young when Henry VIII married her, she was already experienced, and she found the ageing, dropsical King physically repellent. Nothing in her upbringing had conditioned her to caution, and she quickly turned her attention from the King to a handsome young man of his Court, Thomas Culpeper. Inevitably, servant gossip brought the girl's past sexual encounters to light, and worse followed when her liaison with Culpeper was betrayed. Henry, on his return to Hampton Court, at once had both parties arrested, confining Culpeper in the Tower and his wife, Catherine, to her rooms in Wolsey's palace.

The young Queen was by now in a state of near hysteria, for the fate of her cousin, Anne, must have been clear in her mind. She herself was only nineteen and it was inconceivable that she should die. Death was for the old, the decrepit, the senile, not for the young and beautiful, not for her lover, Culpeper. And not for her.

Had she been able to see Henry and plead for her life, perhaps she might have saved it, but there were factions at Court which wanted to destroy the powerful Howard influence. Obstacles were put in the way of any reconciliation and Catherine's terror drove her to desperate action. Knowing the King's routine, she was determined to reach him when he was attending service in the Chapel Royal to which the palace's long gallery gave access. Her own rooms opened off this gallery and all she needed to do was to break from her guards, run along the corridor to the chapel and gain admittance to the royal pew in which the King would be at prayer. Once in his presence she was sure of her ability to win his forgiveness.

She duly made the attempt and actually reached the chapel door, hammering on it frantically and crying out to her husband within, begging him to see her. But by then the guards had caught her and begun to drag her back from its threshold, screaming and sobbing; back down the gallery to her own rooms, which she would only leave again for that sinister fortress, the Tower. Inside the chapel Henry, immobile and cold, listened to her anguished shrieks.

Catherine Howard died on the block on 13 February 1542. She was just twenty. Since then, from time to time, her wild flight down the long gallery has been re-enacted, and on many occasions her frantic screams have been heard, as they were when the guards hauled her away for the last time. Many later residents in the vast house have heard these sounds, and not a few have actually seen the figure in white, its hair long and loose upon its shoulders, as it glides rapidly along the gallery.

I myself when visiting Hampton Court some years ago felt a sensation of extreme coldness at the door of the Chapel Royal, and the sense of an almost physical barrier between gallery and chapel

The Long Gallery at Hampton Court, said to be haunted by the ghost of the unfortunate Catherine Howard, later executed on the orders of Henry VIII. On many occasions her screams have been heard in this gallery.

opposite
Jane Seymour, third wife to Henry VIII. She died at Hampton Court twelve days after giving birth to a son, and her ghost, dressed in white and bearing a lighted candle, has been seen in the Palace.

was so strong that an effort of will was needed to move through it and on into the chapel. Just so does intense human emotion tend to register in an area, leaving an imprint powerful enough to be almost tangible.

A particularly striking aspect of this phantom is that when it is seen, it disappears almost immediately, so that there is no time for more than a brief observance of detail. I do not know of anyone who has seen and recognized the apparition's face, though Catherine Howard's is well known from her portrait, which shows the full sensuous mouth of the Howards, also inherited by Anne Boleyn. Catherine's face does not have Anne's sharp intelligence of eye, however, nor her wariness.

There are psychic traces, too, of Catherine's predecessor in Henry's affection; his 'poor, pretty little Jane'. Jane Seymour had been a lady-in-waiting of *her* predecessor, Anne Boleyn, and even during Anne's lifetime had begun to be courted by the King. History reports that Jane was a quiet girl and she seems to have shown some kindness to the King's young daughters, Mary and Elizabeth. However, she was not averse to betraying her mistress,

under pressure, and Queen Anne could hardly have been unaware of the direction in which her husband's gipsy eye was wandering.

Yet Jane, once Queen, was to enjoy the position for only a year, until the birth of her much-desired son, Edward. She died twelve days later at Hampton Court, to the devastation of Henry who had found her companionable and docile. He was, however, delighted with his boy, for now at last the succession was guaranteed by a legitimate male heir. His other children, the young Mary and little Elizabeth retreated to second and third in the succession respectively.

Although Queen Jane shared her husband's throne for so short a time, something in her tenure of it, or in her life at Hampton Court, apparently caused a psychic imprint to remain, for her wraith has many times been seen in the neighbourhood of the Queen's rooms, often passing through the silver stick gallery and down the stairs. Always the appearance is the same — that of a woman dressed in white, who moves soundlessly bearing in her hand a lighted candle, its flame unflickering and steady. Peter Underwood reports that there have been enough such sightings in recent times to cause servants to leave on the ghost's account. But why the apparition should appear in this particular guise — which suggests night attire — and at this venue, is not known.

A well-authenticated ghost at Hampton Court is one who seems to have the slightest of reasons for haunting at all. She was in life, a certain Mistress Sibell (or Sybil) Penn, appointed foster-mother to the little Prince Edward after Queen Jane's death, and eventually to become his nurse. As part of her duties she must often have needed to go to her spinning-wheel to make the fine thread for her charge's baby clothes, and she does, indeed, seem to have been an exemplary royal servant in every way. Several years after Edward VI's own death, Queen Elizabeth thought highly enough of Mistress Penn to grant her a pension and residence in Hampton Court. Both Queen and nurse suffered an attack of smallpox at the same time in 1562, but while the monarch recovered, the old servant died. She was buried in the church of St Mary's, Hampton, where her body remained until the building was demolished in the 1820s. Afterwards her tomb seems to have been desecrated, and it is from this point that her semblance has been seen in the neighbourhood of her former home.

J.A. Brooks reports a resident in one of Hampton Court's Grace and Favour apartments being awakened one night by someone bending over her bed and peering into her face. The woman, a lady of strong character, demanded what the interloper wanted, to which the latter replied that she needed a home. The occupant of the bed pointed out that she herself owned bed and bedroom and there was no room for strangers. At which point Mistress Penn (for it was thought to have been she) disappeared. Others have seen

opposite
Drawing of a spinning-wheel from a nineteenth-century engraving.

this apparition, particularly in Tennis Court Lane and near the terrace of the great house, and from time to time have heard the hum of a spinning wheel expertly operated, occasionally accompanied by the low mutter of a female voice.

In the nineteenth century a family named Ponsonby, then occupying Sibell Penn's old rooms in the palace, complained of hearing the spinner and her wheel. When investigations were at last undertaken a sealed room was discovered which was found to contain an old spinning-wheel, with the floor beneath it badly worn by the treadle's constant use.

Since then Mistress Penn, a tall figure in a long grey cloak or dress with a hood, has been seen many times, its identity being established by a marked resemblance to the effigy on Sibell Penn's tomb. 'She' also appeared to Princess Frederica of Hanover, who, in describing the figure, gave an accurate picture of Penn's tomb effigy. In recent times this seems to have been the most persistent of the many ghosts of the palace.

However, apart from these, the main historical hauntings by the very makers of history, there are a number of minor psychic echoes in this magnificent monument to human ambition and aspiration.

The gracefully colonnaded Fountain Court was formerly haunted by the ghosts of two cavaliers, frequently seen in broad daylight. One of the percipients was a Lady Hildyard, living in an apartment overlooking the Court in the mid-nineteenth century, who not only saw the two apparitions on several occasions, but complained of unaccountable tapping noises in the area. Eventually the matter was referred to the Lord Chamberlain, but characteristically no immediate action appeared to result. However, in 1871, workmen excavating in Fountain Court near Lady Hildyard's apartments, discovered skeletons which were thought to be those of two cavaliers, Lord Francis Villiers and a colleague, killed in a Civil War skirmish and hastily buried. Whatever their original identity, the bones were removed and decently interred elsewhere, since when there have been no further reported sightings.

A reliable but quite inexplicable sighting was reported in 1907 by a police constable of long experience. He was on duty at the East Front of the palace one February night, and had before him a longish shift which would not end until 6.00 a.m. the following morning. According to his report the constable was standing alone by the main gates, facing in the direction of the Home Park, when he noticed a group of people coming towards him along the Ditton Walk. He was surprised to see such a number of folk in the garden at so late an hour on a winter's evening, but concluded that the two men and seven or nine ladies must have attended a party in nearby Ditton. All were in evening dress, and it was reasonable to assume they were returning home to their respective palace apartments. The constable noted no sound save for what he took to be the

muted rustle of dresses.

The group approached to within a dozen yards of the officer, who by this time had turned to open the gates to allow them into the Fountain Court beyond. However, the party had now altered direction and begun moving towards the Flower Pot Gate of the house. As it did so, its members changed position and fell into processional order, the men leading and the women falling in, two by two, behind them. Then even as the policeman watched, the whole little assembly appeared, as he put it, 'to melt into thin air'. The fact he seemed to find most disturbing was that the final event happened within nine yards of where he stood on the open gravel walk before the palace. Unable to believe his eyes, he ran to the spot, but in spite of looking in various directions, could see nothing to account for the group's disappearance.

One of the intriguing factors about this sighting is the possible identity of the persons concerned. Were they ancient or modern in origin? The 'processionalization' suggests an old and courtly tradition. But if the constable had been observing Tudor, Stuart or Hanoverian courtiers would not the fact have been plain in their dress? He assumed, however, that 'they' were wearing evening dress of his own period. However, although women's evening dress of Edwardian times might have appeared little different from

Fountain Court, Hampton Court, haunted by the ghosts of two cavaliers.

Home Park, Hampton Court. A whole group of ghosts was once seen in this park.

female costume of certain earlier periods, male contemporary evening attire bore no resemblance to anything earlier than about 1830. So to which period did the parading phantoms belong? An unanswerable question. Unless, that is, some later observer should chance to see this elegant procession, and in doing so recognize the costume.

The other curious feature is that the observer should have been able to distinguish the group at all. It was a dark February night. How could the policeman have seen these people distinctly enough either to observe their dress or to count their numbers? Unless the rooms nearby were lit, and threw the glow of lamp– or gaslight across the pathways. Apparently a 'one-off' haunting, this, and curiously tantalizing.

Peter Underwood, whose knowledge of Hampton Court is sound, reports that the actor Leslie Finch, after a performance of *Twelfth Night* at the palace, was walking towards one of its many doorways, accompanied by a then grace-and-favour resident, Lady Grant. Finch noticed what he took to be an actress, wearing a grey Tudor costume, walking towards them. Since she seemed bent on a collision course, he moved aside, but as the woman passed him, he

100

felt a sensation of extreme coldness and a feeling that his skin had suddenly become 'stiff like parchment'. His companion, glancing at him, asked why he had moved so abruptly; it was only then that he realized Lady Grant had seen nothing, although she, too, had felt a passing chill in the air. Finch's 'Tudor grey figure' had not been of flesh and blood, but of some other stuff entirely.

Son et Lumière performances, by contrast with genuine drama, are intended to recreate a little of a place's history, evoke something of its ancient, intrinsic magic. The organizers of one such performance at Hampton Court, however, bargained for rather less than they got.

As far as they knew, the cast consisted of the elements of Sound and Light only. Had live actors been employed, the latter would certainly have expected payment at standard Equity rates. It was a surprise, therefore, to one member of the audience to see a figure dressed as Cardinal Wolsey walking through one of the palace gateways in mid-performance. The watcher wrote later to the producer, pointing out that an actor playing Wolsey had no business in this type of production. Which surprised the producer, as no actor had been playing the Cardinal. The man had apparently

Hampton Court Palace, Middlesex, one of the most haunted of Royal residences. (Tudor West Front)

101

The Great Hall at
Hampton Court. Its roof
timbers bear the Royal
coats of arms of Henry
VIII and Anne Boleyn.

seen the *real* Cardinal Wolsy, in his apparitional, non-material form.

Underwood lists several other ghosts at the great palace, including a monk, a ghostly dog on the King's staircase, a period figure in clerical garments near the tiltyard, and supposedly the ghosts of Derham and Thomas Culpeper, lovers of Catherine Howard.

A house of such size and splendour, such long and emotionally charged history, must have retained many imprints of those who have lived within its ambience, and the secrets of their loves, hates and fears. If emotion, strongly and positively felt, is the factor which produces such 'records' in material objects, then Hampton Court Palace should have invisible cassettes in every wall and window, rafter and rooftree. If we only knew how to switch on each individual 'recorder', we might re-learn history from direct observation. As it is, a considerable number of people now have some idea of Catherine Howard's possible reaction when her infidelity was revealed to her husband.

opposite
The King's Staircase at
Hampton Court. A
ghostly dog has been
glimpsed on these stairs.

HOLYROODHOUSE
Edinburgh

Many visitors to Scotland must be puzzled by the name of Holyroodhouse and curious as to its origin. Like several ancient names, it originated with a legend, whose substance is this. On 14 September 1128, David, King of Scots, while staying in Edinburgh Castle, was persuaded to go hunting after attending Mass, though against the wishes of his Confessor, the English Monk Alwin.

Heedless, the King pursued a fine stag through the valley of Abergare (the modern Canongate) until nearing Salisbury Crag, when the animal turned, charged the King and unhorsed him, at the same time inflicting on him a thigh wound. The King grappled with the beast, seizing a crucifix which had miraculously appeared between its antlers. The stag left the cross in the monarch's hands and bounded away towards a nearby spring of water.

That night in a dream David was instructed to build 'a house for Canons devoted to the Cross'. He duly erected an Abbey near the stag's spring, and named it the Abbey of the Holy Rood (an ancient term for Christ's cross), creating Alwin its first Abbot.

This is an attractive tale, but it is similar to others connected with medieval Christian sites in Europe, and they would seem to have a shared origin.

The Abbey, in common with other monastic houses, had its own guest house, used regularly by the Kings of Scots in their passage to and from their royal Burgh of Edinburgh. In time the guest house became an official royal residence fit to receive the designation of palace. And eventually, its purlieus became incorporated into the city of Edinburgh.

In the fourteenth and fifteenth centuries parliaments were frequently held at Holyrood and James II of Scotland was born, crowned, married and buried there. James III often stayed in the place and had his queen, Margaret of Denmark, crowned in the abbey in 1469. This King was defeated and killed in battle by his son's supporters, and when that son was crowned James IV, he determined to revitalize and unite Scotland. It was he who transformed the old Abbey guesthouse into a palatial royal home and began work on the fine north-west tower which was to be the scene of historic violence in his granddaughter's reign. It was this statesmanlike and chivalrous James who, in an attempt to secure peace between Scotland and 'the auld enemy', England, married Henry VII's daughter, Margaret Tudor, bringing her to live in Holyrood's newly-built north-west tower. Although Margaret did not care for the country of her adoption, after her husband's death at Flodden, she remarried and continued to live in it.

It was her son, James V (he who had such an unreasonable hatred of the Douglas clan), who completed the north-west tower so that both king's and queen's apartments were provided.

When it came to marriage, James V chose from the princesses of Scotland's traditional ally, France. He first selected the slight,

Mary, Queen of Scots as a young woman (c.1560). Portrait attributed to F. Clovet.

delicate Madeleine, Francis I's daughter, but after two months of marriage and the Scottish climate, the frail girl died. James, undiscouraged (the Stuarts were prone to stubbornness), then selected another Frenchwoman, Mary of Guise, a widow, and made of sterner stuff. She became the mother of the Queen to whom, more than any other, legends would attach: Mary, Queen of Scots.

It is with Mary that Holyrood is most associated in the popular mind. In her, Stuart charm would come to full fruition and she was to lay its spell on all who came within her orbit.

Mary's father, James V, died a week after her birth, and the child was only eight months old when she was crowned at Stirling Castle

HENRICVS * SCOTORVM · REX · ARNLEY · DE · DOMINVS

**Henry Stuart, Lord
Darnley. Artist unknown.**

on 9 September 1543. It had originally been proposed that Mary wed Henry VIII's young son, Edward, but Mary of Guise wished to avoid an alliance with England, preferring to renew ties with her own native land. As a result, at the age of fifteen the young Queen of Scots was married to Francis II of France, only to be widowed a year later. She then returned to Scotland to take up her royal responsibilities there.

In England Elizabeth I was without an heir and showed no sign of marrying. Mary of Scotland was the nearest claimant to the English throne through her Tudor grandmother, and although Elizabeth found this a distasteful solution she was forced to accept it as a possibility. However, whether deliberately or accidentally, the English Queen was instrumental in Mary's own foolish choice of a husband, when she sent the unstable young Lord Darnley from her own court to that of her Scottish cousin. Mary, also a cousin of Darnley, fell in love with the arrogant youth and married him in the Chapel Royal at Holyrood. From that point, Henry Stuart, Lord Darnley, was granted equal rank with his wife and became ever more demanding, desiring full kingly authority. He appreciated that if the Queen bore a male child, he, Darnley would become his own son's subject. But if that child should die — or fail to be born — Darnley himself might ultimately attain the supreme position.

Mary had a Piedmontese musician in her retinue, David Rizzio, 'a merry fellow and a good musician'. She drew him into her immediate circle and, needing a friend she could trust, made Rizzio her secretary. Darnley, true to his reputation for immaturity, was furiously jealous. Perhaps it was from this emotion that the idea stemmed to murder the Italian. Or perhaps there was some hope that a bloody deed carried out in the Queen's presence might produce both a miscarriage and her own death. The motives are unclear now. The facts, however, are not.

The Protestant nobles of Scotland fearing their Catholic Queen was about to seize their lands, had little to lose by disposing of one monarch in favour of another.

Mary's apartments were on the second floor of the James IV tower, and consisted of two main rooms and two small antechambers. Darnley occupied the suite below hers (similar in plan) and the two were connected by a privy staircase which reached Mary's bedroom. One of the two small rooms was used as a dressing-room, the other as a supper room, and on the night of 9 March 1566, the Queen and five guests, including David Rizzio, dined there, the intention being afterwards to listen to music and play cards. The Queen was six months pregnant, and leading a quiet life. Her husband, on the other hand, frequented the taverns and low night life of Edinburgh, coming rarely to see his wife.

Mary cannot, therefore, have expected what occurred. It is not difficult to imagine the scene: the Queen, tall and graceful even in pregnancy, her rich copper hair (a Tudor inheritance) smooth under the heart-shaped cap, her few women seated about her, with the Italian, Rizzio, about to play to this beautiful woman whose friend he had become. What his feelings were for the Queen can only be surmised. Perhaps admiration and gratitude; perhaps more. Those who knew Mary well found many affectionate names for her.

The scene was set then for a placid evening, when abruptly there came the sound of running footsteps on the stairs from Darnley's apartments, and almost immediately he himself threw open the door of the supper room and looked inside — presumably to see

who was present. Having satisfied himself that Rizzio was there, he withdrew. The Queen had no time to express her surprise at this unexpected visit, before several armed nobles forced their way into the room led by the grim and half-demented old Patrick, Earl of Ruthven. 'Let it please Your Majesty,' he said 'that yonder man David come forth of your privy chamber where he hath been

David Rizzio, Mary's Italian secretary, murdered in Holyroodhouse in 1566.

111

overlong.' Rizzio, foreseeing the men's purpose, fell to his knees and clung to the Queen's skirts, crying 'Sauvez ma vie, Madame! Sauvez ma vie!' Mary did what she could to protect him, but the lords had wound themselves up to a frenzy of violence, and the only result of the Queen's intervention was to provoke a torrent of abuse from Ruthven, who accused her of adultery with Rizzio, even suggesting that he might be her child's father. At that point Rizzio was dragged from the Queen's feet, out of the supper room, through the audience chamber to the top of the main staircase. In these few yards he was stabbed more than fifty times. As a last contemptuous gesture the dagger belonging to the King Consort, Darnley, though not used by him, was left in the body of the musician. It was a sign of official approval by Darnley of the murder.

There seems no doubt that the killing was an attempt to remove both Mary and her child. As neat and nasty an assassination attempt as has ever been made.

But Mary kept both her courage and her presence of mind, though no doubt expecting at any moment to receive the lords' daggers herself. Although her mental state immediately after this brutal event can be imagined, and her feeling of revulsion against her husband, she needed Darnley until she could extricate herself from Holyroodhouse and the presence of Ruthven and his fellows. That night she left with Darnley by the servants' quarters, riding the five-hour journey to Dunbar Castle; but not before vowing to her waiting women that she would avenge Rizzio's murder.

Three months later she gave birth to her son, James, in Edinburgh Castle, thus ensuring the succession in both Scotland and England.

Eight months later, in February 1567, Darnley caught smallpox, and because of the danger to the baby was persuaded by Mary to convalesce alone in the old provost's house at Kirk o'Field. Mary visited him there on the evening of 9 February, but returned to Holyroodhouse the same night in order to attend a wedding. During that night the Kirk o'Field house was blown up and the King Consort's body was found the next morning in the grounds. He had been strangled.

It has always been assumed that Mary had authorized the removal of Darnley, and that the murder was carried out by James Hepburn, Earl of Bothwell. It was Bothwell who became the Queen of Scots' third husband, a scandal which was to lose her her throne, and result in the long, dreary English imprisonment which ended at Fotheringhay.

Perhaps everything that occurred at Holyroodhouse after Mary's departure is bound to seem anti-climactic. James I (and VI) used the palace until called to the throne of England, returning only once to visit it. Charles I came to Holyrood for his coronation in the Abbey

A reconstruction of the assassination of David Rizzio.

Church, and once again when the seeds of Civil War were already sprouting. Charles II never entered the palace, though he did institute repairs and extensive alterations there. Thereafter, although occasionally visited by royalty, Holyrood ceased to be regularly inhabited. Prince Charles Edward Stuart (Bonnie Prince Charlie) bent on winning the British crown back for the Old Pretender, his father, visited the home of his ancestors, and appeared at one of Holyrood's windows to acknowledge excited Jacobite cheers. The day ended with a magnificent ball held in the palace's long gallery. The Prince delayed long enough at Holyrood, creating a glittering court around himself, to give George II of England time to organize his forces. Prince Charles Edward reached Derby, but not London, and after his long retreat north was eventually destroyed as a political force at Culloden.

Knowing the story of a place and the details of its history are one thing; visiting it and interviewing the people who live and work there, another. I went to Holyrood, knowing its reputation and the predominance of the Mary, Queen of Scots, episodes, with anticipation and interest. In the event, I had rather more fulfilment of both than I had bargained for.

A number of Holyrood's working personnel had experiences to report, though since they were canny Scots they were not unduly keen to talk.

In the year 1976 or 1977, one of the senior staff had been in Darnley's audience chamber with a colleague at the end of a normal tourist day. This, the main room of the King's suite, is handsome, altered since Darnley's day by Charles II's restructuring, though with its basic proportions little changed. In one corner of the room is the staircase leading up to Mary's audience chamber (King's and Queen's suites were originally identical in layout and one above the other), and the convex shape of the wall above the door giving on to the stairs indicates the presence of the turret.

The officers were alone in the room when the senior of the pair chanced to glance across to the stairway door, which was closed. However, at its foot is a space of about an inch between it and the floor, and he thought he saw a movement beyond — as though a shadow had passed across the space, suggesting that someone was behind the door. He assumed, not unreasonably, that a tourist had either accidentally or deliberately lingered beyond the time of closing. He ran across to the door and pulled it open, but the space behind and the stairs leading upward were empty. Both men then thoroughly searched the stairway, but without result.

On another occasion the same senior official was conducting a party of tourists around the palace and the group had paused in the Queen's bedroom. This room has an unusual tempera frieze and the official chanced to gaze at it while speaking of the room's history. In mid-sentence he hesitated, for he had noticed what seemed to be a patch of mist emerging from the frieze. Unwilling to draw attention to the phenomenon, however, he pressed on with his lecture, and when he glanced at the frieze again the curious mist patch had vanished.

Yet again, towards dusk on an autumn day of 1976 or 1977, this same warden had been conducting a group around the palace and, as part of the tour, they entered the Queen's bedchamber. The official at once felt something 'strange, cold, not quite right about it,' and suggested that they should leave, as he felt exceedingly uncomfortable there. The tourists' reaction is not recorded.

When HM The Queen is in residence, the Household uses the James IV wing (the Mary wing) as offices. Several people working at such times have seen a 'lady in grey' (identity not known) standing in Mary's audience chamber near the entrance to one of the staircases. The figure is always indistinct, as though perceived from a distance, and its facial features are not distinguishable.

Later I spoke to a security officer, an ex-soldier, as are many of the official guardians of royal homes, who told me that on several occasions when on night duty in the building he has felt very uneasy in one particular area, the long gallery. This gallery, a fine room of beautiful proportions, is filled with some singularly bad paintings by Jacob de Witt, a Dutch artist employed by Charles II on a hack basis to paint portraits of all eighty-nine Scottish monarchs. Since the features of most of the early incumbents were unknown and since Charles was paying an average of only £2 per painting, the poor quality of De Witt's handiwork is hardly surprising. However, the gallery is not, one assumes, haunted by the disgruntled artist.

The security officer has experienced a strong sensation, from time to time, either that someone was following him along the gallery or preceding him. And four times in the last three years he has heard the sound of footsteps in this area; again, sometimes before, sometimes behind where he himself patrolled. The occasional sense of coldness is less disturbing to him, though often it occurs when the house's central heating is in full operation.

This official has never actually seen anything at any time, although he told me an interesting anecdote of a window-cleaner who was less fortunate. This man, the owner of a window-cleaning contracting business, regularly cleaned the palace's windows and the work must have had some similarities with the painting of the Forth Bridge a few miles away. One autumn day the man was cleaning the windows of the long gallery and had pulled down the top half of a particular window when, framed in the other side of it he saw a human face, wearing a stiff white ruff around its neck and a black cloak, the collar of which was turned up: a description which fits typical sixteenth-century male costume.

The window-cleaner was so alarmed by what he had seen that he hurriedly came down his ladder, climbed into his car and drove away. He neither returned later to complete the job nor has been seen at the palace since. The window-cleaning contract eventually went elsewhere. There do not seem to have been any subsequent sightings of the face at the window.

I spent two-and-a-half days touring Holyroodhouse and talking to various members of its personnel. Yet when all the information is gathered, both of a place's history and its inhabitants' experiences, a certain amount of weight must be given to one's own impression of it. If this is true as a general principle, it is particularly so when the subject of investigation is parapsychology.

I had been told several years ago by an eminent member of the present Royal Family that 'the Rizzio room' had 'a terrible atmosphere'. My own experience bore this out. I found it quite impossible to stay in this, the small supper or supping room for more than a few minutes at a time, and matters were made worse by the fact

that the sense of horror which afflicts it appears to be concentrated in one single area, the left hand side near the entrance door. The sensation is so intense that it almost seems to have *weight* — as though the very air were thicker at that spot. It is also of the kind that the longer one stays in the room the worse the feeling of oppression becomes.

Melville's contemporary record of the murder stated that the room in which Mary, Rizzio and others were eating supper was a 12 foot by 12 foot chamber. One of the two antechambers in the Queen's suite (at present occupied by a member of the staff as a restroom and therefore not accessible to the public) has precisely these proportions, but the second room, traditionally known as the supper room, is considerably smaller. Yet when one of the senior officials and I examined it together, it was obvious that it had once been much wider (it is still about 12 foot *long*), and the original proportions before alteration would have made it a square room, thus meeting Melville's description.

The floor level in all the rooms on this floor has been raised by about two feet.

The staircases, too, are ambiguous, but the older of the two — its upper portion not now accessible to the public — would certainly have served as a sudden entrance for Darnley; and his supporters

116

could have used both this and the other contemporaneous flight, now glazed off and with no public access.

As for the brass plaque on the floor of the Queen's audience chamber, believed to mark the spot where the body of the Italian was left, there is nothing to prove its authenticity as the place where he actually died. The unfortunate man would have had to be dragged from the supper room across the Queen's bedroom *and* the audience chamber. He could have died anywhere *en route*. What does support the plaque-marked spot as his final resting-place is that Mary is said to have had a partition erected to ceiling height to shut off from her view this scene of appalling memory. There are still signs in the original oak ceiling that such a partition once existed, though it has long since been removed.

The main horror, though, remains where it must always have been: in the supper room. And whether that horror were Rizzio's or Mary's is impossible to tell.

At the end of my notes on this piece of research, I have written:

An ugly rather than a romantic tale. But many of these ghost stories are. This palace is all stone, and would be a good recorder. Glad I am not living in it.

A view of Kensington Palace, London. The statue is of Queen Victoria.

KENSINGTON PALACE

London

George II, like numerous other eldest sons, was unable to get along with his father, George I of Hanover and England. When the son eventually succeeded to the throne it became apparent that he did not much care for his adopted land, either, and would have preferred to return to Hanover. Beggars in this case were unable to be choosers, for Britain was a greater plum as a domain than the small German state could ever be. George II remained in England, residing in Kensington Palace and enjoying the comfortable life of the wealthy and powerful.

Kensington House as it was originally known, was bought by William III at the instigation of his wife, Mary II, as an alternative to the somewhat remote (from London) Hampton Court, and the

118

Monarch paid the Earl of Nottingham 18,000 guineas for it. The attractive brick villa then was handed over to Christopher Wren to transform into a palace.

The building lay on the western side of Hyde Park with its population of deer, had large gardens of its own and was adjacent to the pretty country village of Kensington and neighbouring farms. Mary was in a great hurry to move into her new home and ceaselessly chivvied Wren, both at Hampton Court and Kensington, to hurry his reconstructions so that the royal couple might soon take possession. The consequences of her impatience were that at both venues the work was hurried, causing roofs to collapse and workmen to be killed. However, although the venture started badly, William and Mary appear to have been happy in their new palace — into which they moved just before Christmas 1689, in spite of the fact that builders and scaffolding were still much in evidence everywhere. The diarist, Evelyn, seeing the place early in 1690, found it 'a patched building, but with the garden . . . a very sweet villa.' There was one innovation: a new road was made through the park, wide enough for three coaches to drive abreast, and at regular intervals along the route posts were set for lamps which were lit every evening when the Court was in residence. The way to Kensington was noted for its attraction for highwaymen.

The interior of Kensington Palace soon became crammed with the best of the several royal art collections, and contained much work by the Flemish and Italian masters. The Queen, who had acquired a fine collection of Chinese porcelain during her years in Holland, set it up in Kensington House, thus starting a new fashion craze.

Although William and Mary left no great mark on English politics, they began a pattern of royal domesticity which, give or take a few exceptions, still persists today.

George II, distant cousin of the monarchs of the House of Orange, and second ruler of the Hanoverian line, came to the throne in 1727. He was to reign for thirty-three years, and for most of that time heartily wished himself back in Hanover. Unlike his father, he spoke reasonable English though with a strong German accent.

It was his misfortune that England became involved in yet another of its many European wars during his reign, and he was the last British monarch to lead his troops in battle, at Dettingen. In the New World, America was fighting for her independence from England, and France and Britain were embroiled in bitter conflict over possession of Canada. George II, as well as his subjects, must have been in a continual state of war-alertness, therefore, and it is not surprising that Kensington Palace's haunting apparently arises from this fact.

During his last illness the King was confined to his rooms at Kensington, but even *in extremis* his mind was occupied by the

Kensington Palace, London. The ghost of King George II has been seen looking from one of the Palace windows towards the weather-vane. (The statue in shadow is of William III.)

King George II, who
spent his last days
confined to a room in
Kensington Palace.

The Orangery,
Kensington Palace.

need to have news of his troops.

The month was October 1760 and he was awaiting important despatches from Hanover. The equinoctial gales were blowing in full force and all ships bound from the Continent to Britain were pinned in port by the fierce westerlies. As the King's health rapidly declined, and he felt his time ebbing, he became more and more impatient for news. Time after time he struggled from his bed to the window, looking out at the palace weather-vane to see if the wind had changed. It remained resolutely in the west, and on each occasion George would groan 'Vy t'on't dey com?'

When eventually the wind veered and the ships crept out of port towards England, it was too late for the King. He had died on 25 October, to be succeeded by his grandson.

George II's state of anxiety must have been strong enough to register on his surroundings, however, for at intervals since that time the wan face of the monarch has been seen looking from a window of the palace towards the weather-vane. It is even said that his voice has sometimes been heard, asking its futile and heavily accented question.

Echoes, these, with no living, active spirit behind them. Mere echoes of past emotion, which at the time of their existence some part of Kensington Palace absorbed into itself and held. We do not fully understand how or why this process operates, but no doubt its discovery is only a matter of time, patience and persistent inquiry.

THE CASTLE OF MEY

Caithness

The most northerly castle in Britain lies six miles from John O'Groats, built in the wild moorland county of Caithness by that county's Earl in the sixteenth century.

When Queen Elizabeth, the Queen Mother, found it, she had been widowed a year and was taking a holiday in her native Scotland as the guest of old friends, Commander and Lady Doris Vyner.

The castle, known as Barrogill, though originally called the Castle of Mey, had little to recommend it. Its main attraction was that it was small, isolated, and looked out over the tide races of Pentland Firth to the green low outline of the Orkneys beyond, with the Stroma cliffs defining the distance. The castle's physical condition was abysmal and would have daunted the stoutest heart. Its roof was collapsing, it was innocent of any form of heating and the garden resembled a cross between Arctic tundra and the Canadian wilderness. Local rumour was that the building would be demolished, thus putting an end to its four hundred years of history.

The Queen Mother, however, does not discourage easily. Having lost the central pivot of her life, she needed some immediate purpose, a work which would occupy and absorb her energies for a while. Perhaps the crumbling little building provided focus, or struck some emotional chord in her. In the event, she bought it and restored it over a period of three years at a cost of some £40,000, taking possession at last in 1955.

According to Jean Goodman's interesting account in *Royal Scotland*, the Castle of Mey was originally built and owned by the Sinclairs, descendants of Viking raiders on Scotland's northern coasts, and it remained in their possession until the 15th Earl, dying young and unmarried, irresponsibly willed it away from the family and to a former Cambridge friend.

Now after years of dereliction it is once more a home, being furnished in pleasant light colours, and with many of the former Sinclair possessions rescued from local antique shops. The periods vary from Queen Anne to Regency, with a little Victoriana added for flavour. The gardens, too, are rejuvenated, growing flowers, fruit, vegetables and herbs for the owner's use.

When the Queen Mother is in residence she is likely to be visited by children, grandchildren and great-grandchildren, and on the completion of Mey's restoration the royal yacht *Britannia* anchored in the little bay which serves the castle, bearing the family on a visit to this new royal property.

Aerial view of the Castle of Mey.

The original owners, the Sinclairs, left more than an attractive half-ruin behind them, however. Like most powerful Scottish families, they had known their share of violence and bloodshed. One heir to the Earldom in the sixteenth century was imprisoned by his bloodthirsty father and tortured by his younger brother whom he, in turn, tried to strangle in his desperation, and whose death resulted from the attempt.

But it is not from this period that Mey's single psychic echo originates. A daughter of the castle in later times, Lady Fanny Sinclair, unwisely fell in love with a good-looking groom in her father's employ. When the attachment was discovered the unlucky lad was summarily dismissed and immediately departed for London; closely followed by Lady Fanny.

However, this was not an era of self-determination in the choice of partners, nor, at least in Great Britain, of marrying out of one's class. The girl was forcibly brought back to her home by her family, whereupon she threw herself from a castle window and was killed. According to an account by James Wentworth Day, her ghost is thought still to haunt the scene of her death.

The Castle of Mey, to whom the owner has restored its original name in addition to much else, will no doubt withstand a small haunting as it has withstood the rest of its varied history.

The Castle of Mey, Caithness. Lady Fanny Sinclair
threw herself to her death from one of its windows.

NETHER LYPIATT MANOR

Gloucestershire

If you travel into Gloucestershire looking for the village of Nether Lypiatt, you will search in vain. There is no village. Nether Lypiatt is the name of an estate which was originally part of a larger one now split into three.

But there is a manor house at Nether Lypiatt, a square, Georgian building on seventeenth-century foundations, which exudes a rather formidable air, its two rows of front windows and attic dormers looking across a small square garden with a gravelled courtyard-cum-driveway before it.

In the late nineteen-seventies Nether Lypiatt Manor was the property of Simon and Suna Boyle, but according to a *Daily Express* report of 28 January 1984, the couple must have felt less than comfortable there for at one time they called in a priest to deal with certain apparent hauntings of the house and garden. What exactly took place during his visit is not clear, but the clergyman is said to have 'found things in the house' which he 'did not like', and to have advised the owners on methods of dealing with them. In the newspaper report, neither the unpleasant 'things' nor the proposed countermeasures were specified. Mrs Boyle, when asked on an earlier occasion about possible ghosts at the Manor, had simply refused to comment.

There are, however, persistent rumours of hauntings at this place, and when the house was purchased by Prince and Princess Michael of Kent in 1981, a buzz of excited speculation stirred the hives of Fleet Street. A leading exorcist in the Church of England had been asked to undertake a ceremony in the house, stated one report. 'A bizarre religious ceremony', announced another, going on to say that two priests had been involved, one Roman Catholic, the other Anglican, and that the house's owners had also taken part. As for the identity of the ghost, if ghosts there were, the guesses were various. One reporter in 1981 had stated that Mrs Suna Boyle had seen 'a frock-coated figure' seated at her dinner-table, though no details were given as to when or on how many occasions. The rash of 1984 accounts seems to have been ignorant of the frock-coated fellow and instead concentrated on the figure of a spectral young blacksmith who appears as regular as the calendar each January, riding a white horse. Yet a third rumour hinted at a strange Woman in White who occasionally visits the place and is said to haunt the grounds.

Looked at objectively, such a wealth of rumours, speculation and reputed attempts at counteracting whatever (if anything) was going on at Nether Lypiatt, suggested that no one had much idea whether the stories were fact or fancy. But agitations of this nature concern-

opposite
Nether Lypiatt Manor, Gloucestershire, now the home of Prince and Princess Michael of Kent. Its grounds are said to be haunted by a White Lady and also by the ghost of a young blacksmith, hanged by a previous owner for not completing the gates to the courtyard by the time specified.

129

A white horse is another of the ghosts at Nether Lypiatt Manor. (Study of horses' heads, from a painting by J.F. Herring.)

ing a particular place often mean that there have been enough inexplicable occurrences to give rise to the tales. The reports originally may be based on personal experience, but with the passage of time and endless repetition, the basic facts distort and swell. To get as near as possible to the truth one has to go back to the framework.

Nether Lypiatt Manor over the years has had a series of owners, and the ghostly blacksmith seems to have originated with one of these — a certain Judge Charles Coxe, in whose circuit the house was during the seventeenth (or at the latest, eighteenth) century, and who seems to have possessed the house in consequence of his professional duties.

I spoke to a number of local people, who while not belonging to the Lypiatt estate yet lived in the area and had done so for a number of years. They were all familiar with the basic story, and the following facts seem to have been handed down through several generations with little amendment.

When Judge Coxe gained possession of the manor house he ordered a pair of iron gates to be made by the local blacksmith — an excellent craftsman, though young. The Judge, who would seem to have been as ruthless and vicious as the notorious Judge George Jeffreys, announced the date by which he required the gates to be ready. The young smith protested that it was well-nigh impossible to carry out the task within the time limit, but Coxe's response was that if the gates were not completed by the time specified their maker would certainly be hanged. Perhaps the brutal threat was merely meant as a spur to rural tardiness; or perhaps the blacksmith was not convinced of the Judge's serious intentions; for when the deadline (and the Judge) arrived, the gates were not finished, and Coxe, instead of supervising the hanging of his gates, duly hanged the unfortunate blacksmith.

The death, according to legend, took place on 25 January, and annually on or around that date the ghost of the young smith is said to ride a large white horse across the courtyard of Nether Lypiatt Manor.

This is a typical 'anniversary' haunting, and one doubts the exactitude of any haunting of this type; for calendar variations, and the unlikelihood of any type of ghost having knowledge of exact timing, make it highly unlikely. If such anniversary hauntings do tend to occur in the same month as the original drama from which they sprang, then I think the factors of temperature and light have more control of their seasonal recurrence than actual dates.

This would seem to be so in the case of the blacksmith — in which legend local people appear to believe — although at least part of the surroundings have changed since the haunting's inception. The 'courtyard' of the original story is now merely a broad, gravelled driveway which crosses the house front, and it is this area with which the phantom smith is concerned.

Unfortunately for verification, I found no one who had actually seen this spectre, and I suspect that it may by now have died away. If it is indeed recorded electrical impulses which can re-create the scenes of ancient drama, then it is logical to suppose that these will in time become weaker and eventually fade entirely, thus causing any 'haunting' produced to end. And the experience with hauntings of the regular-pattern type is that they do precisely this, although their duration before fading may be anything from a few

131

months to a few centuries. Yet fade eventually, they do.

The other type of haunting, in which the central figure (it usually concerns a figure rather than an event), appears to have liberty of action and varies such actions freely, suggests a living consciousness which has retained the power of decision; in other words, a true ghost, a consciousness or extra-physical energy outside of matter.

As far as Nether Lypiatt is concerned, a much more interesting apparition than the ill-rewarded blacksmith is that of the Grey Lady. Not, as in the rumours regarding the haunting of the grounds, a White Lady. I suspect the latter may be only a dislocation and misdescription of the grey woman of the house.

The story of the Grey Lady I had from several sources, but the most detailed and probably the most accurate account came from a police officer still living and working in the area.

Although the interior of the manor has been known for many years to be haunted by a grey figure, the most recent experience of it occurred when a man working in one of the attics finished his job and began to descend the stairs. He had reached the first floor when he began to feel uneasy. He was convinced that someone was watching him. And worse than that, that whoever it was, was very near. He cast a quick look over his shoulder, not, one supposes, expecting to see anything. There, a few paces behind him on the stairs, stood the figure of a woman, entirely grey, from the shawl she wore over her head with its long ends hanging down, to the hem of her skirt. He began hurriedly to continue his descent. And so did the figure behind him. He rushed down the next flight, but when he turned around the figure was still just behind him. The alarmed man hurried out of the building as quickly as he could, made for the nearest telephone box and 'phoned the local police station.

What he actually believed he had seen we cannot guess, but he reported that he had encountered an intruder within the manor house; someone unauthorized had broken in and he felt the police would want to know.

The constable on duty was less alarmed than his informant, for he recognized the description. 'You've seen the local ghost,' he explained, 'the Grey Lady.' The workman is said to have been reassured, though personally I have my doubts on that score.

This, then, is the most solid of the Nether Lypiatt stories. There is no known historical anecdote to account for the Grey Lady, but she would seem to be closely associated with the house's history, and is almost certainly a former inhabitant, though of what period it is impossible to say without further details of her costume. She appears very rarely or, if the clergy's activities were successful, perhaps not at all now. Yet it was as late as 1984 that Fleet Street cheerfully reported clerical attempts to dislodge the haunting(s).

The gardens of this small manor house have the charm of an unfinished exercise. On one little escarpment overlooking a deep, wooded dell, a series of stone tablets are let into the grass in memory of family dogs of the 1920s and 1930s; each bears an affectionate inscription. A great fig tree grows against the front wall of the house, half embracing it and spreading steadily round the side wall of the garden square. The lawns are non-immaculate and the weeds thrive more happily there than in more dragooned gardens of this type.

Nether Lypiatt has a perfect air of naturalness and of living its life quietly, without interruption.

Newark Castle,
Selkirkshire, owned by
the Duke of Buccleuch,
who took this photograph
of it.

NEWARK CASTLE

Selkirkshire

Several years ago I drove north to Selkirkshire, ostensibly for a touring holiday in the beautiful Lowland country of Scotland, but with an unadmitted intention of looking at one of Montrose's old battlefields, near Selkirk.

Montrose: a name that to all those of Scottish ancestry is a stirrer of the blood, a reminder of great deeds; of valour, nobility and the ideal of chivalry.

James Graham, First Marquis of Montrose, 'The Great Marquis' as posterity has labelled him, was originally a supporter of the Scottish Solemn League and Covenant which sought to restrict Charles I's exercise of absolute royal power. When the Covenanters showed signs of going beyond their initial intention and posing a threat to the King himself, Montrose repudiated them. At heart he was a King's man and would not deny his allegiance to Charles.

When the split between Parliament and monarch became final, the Graham offered his services to raise a Scottish army for the royal cause, and the King eventually made him Captain-General of his army in Scotland.

That army, as it happened, was non-existent, and Montrose was left to raise one however he could. Most of his recruits came from the Highlands, many from clans at loggerheads with the mighty Clan Campbell, whose leader Archibald, Marquis of Argyll, had no love for Montrose, and had earned himself the nickname of King Campbell. Other support came from Macleans and MacDonalds and the latter's kinsmen in Ireland. The bitterness between the Catholic Irish and Protestant Scots might have brought the venture to a standstill before it began, had not Montrose's skill with men and remarkable qualities of leadership not charmed the opponents into a surprising unity.

So began 1645, Montrose's year of miracles, during which he won battle after battle against Covenanting forces generally superior in generalship, for James Graham was a fine soldier and captain, and perhaps the greatest exponent of guerrilla tactics these islands have produced. The little army he commanded for the King played tag with Argyll's Covenanters through the hills and over the moors of the Highlands, throughout autumn and into a fierce white winter. In the depth of which Montrose marched his whole force over the central massif of the Highlands, deep in snow, to fall upon Argyll's personal stronghold Inveraray Castle on Loch Fyne. Argyll clambered aboard his boat and precipitately fled.

The run of miraculous victories lasted exactly a year, then the luck changed. The Irish MacDonalds returned home, the Highlanders turned back to their glens and Montrose's army dwindled to a few hundred men. He was marching across Selkirkshire, bound for the Border, recruiting as he went, when he paused to camp overnight on the meadows of Philiphaugh, in the shadow of Newark Castle. Montrose with his cavalry rode into Selkirk town, and he himself stayed at a small house there, though much against the guidwife's will, for she, along with many Lowlanders, could not forgive Montrose for using the dreaded Catholic Irish to fight good Scots Protestants. The Irish infantry camped three miles away, where the glens of Ettrick and Yarrow meet, in the valley flatland known as Philiphaugh, with water on one side and a steep hill on the other. At the narrow end of the vale and facing the hill, Newark Castle, a Buccleuch stronghold and former royal hunting seat, traditionally belonging to the Queens of Scotland, stood square and formidable, its small courtyard running to the very edge of the escarpment which formed one wall of the valley.

Montrose knew that a large Covenanting force under General David Leslie would shortly have to be faced and dealt with, and he had been discreetly following its movements for some time, wait-

ing to pounce when his own army was strong enough to snatch victory. As far as he knew, Leslie's forces were far to the north of his own troops, in the Forth area.

What he could not know was that a local chieftain, John Stewart, Earl of Traquair, had informed the enemy of Montrose's whereabouts, and Leslie's troops were even now rapidly advancing on Selkirk: the stalker had become the stalked.

The morning of 13 September 1646 dawned into a fog thick with the earth-scents of autumn, and in the valley hollow it was barely possible to see more than six feet ahead. The Royalists sent out scouts, who reported that all was clear, except towards the east, where a few pickets appeared to have been involved in a skirmish with other soldiers. It was assumed that this fracas related to a drunken brawl, whereas in fact the soldiers encountered were the outpost of Leslie's 6,000 strong army. They were not on the Forth but on Montrose's doorstep.

Montrose himself, weary from constant travelling, marching, fighting and hope deferred, had spent a sleepless night in Selkirk, dealing with dispatches to the King, having given orders that he was not to be disturbed. His little army in the haugh was cooking itself a leisurely breakfast in the assurance that the enemy was many miles away.

Leslie, also, was an able Commander. Dividing his forces into two, he cut the Selkirk road and flung his powerful cavalry down the valley on to the unsuspecting Royalists, at that moment assembling for morning parade.

When the news reached Montrose, he and his cavalry leaders raced to the haugh, to find the Irish infantry trapped between the two enemy forces. Montrose, heading a mere hundred horsemen, time and again cut into the enemy lines to relieve the Irish fighting like furies against Leslie's onslaughts. But they were 600 against 6,000 and the conclusion was never in doubt. As John Buchan says in his fine account, Philiphaugh was a massacre*. When only fifty Royalist horse were left and 400 of their infantry lay dead on the field, the Irish surrendered. Montrose, who had shown every sign of intending to die with his men, was dragged from the scene by his friends and persuaded to flee. If he died the King's cause in Scotland must die with him. He gave way and, with a handful of others, cut a road out and over the hills to Tweeddale.

The Irish infantry, who had been promised their lives by Leslie on surrender, were first disarmed and then coldbloodedly slaughtered where they stood, their officers being kept for execution later. Leslie, an honourable soldier, had been overruled by the Church's Ministers who accompanied his troops and who howled for blood as loudly as though they had never seen it. In the name of God and

* *Montrose*, John Buchan.

opposite
Archibald, Marquis of Argyll, nicknamed 'King Campbell'

the Kirk were slaughtered also three hundred women and children, families of the Irishmen, and two hundred camp servants, cooks and horse-boys. The hills were searched for several days thereafter, and any fugitives found were butchered without mercy. They were hanged, had their throats cut, were thrown into rivers and held down with pikes until they drowned. And all in the name of some strange and cruel God worshipped by the Kirk's ordained Ministers. Montrose's year of miracles ended to the sound of Royalist mourning and Covenanting celebration.

When I came to Philiphaugh I did so knowing something of the history of the battle and its outcome, though little of the detail. I had not heard of the incidental slaughter of the innocents or its timing, although aware that the massacre of the troops had taken place somewhere in the narrow end of the valley.

I myself stayed in pleasant, grey-stoned Selkirk town, and in the course of research met a local historian who kindly offered to show me the battlefield. We made an appointment to visit Philiphaugh the following morning.

The valley when we reached it turned out to be excessively narrow at the Newark Castle end, a veritable bottleneck. Any troops caught in that trap would have had no chance of escape. We stood in Newark's crumbling courtyard and gazed out across the vale-head to the high moor opposite, across which James Graham and his handful of men escaped. Almost at our feet, the escarpment on which the castle stood fell sheer to the valley floor beneath us. Little hope of the desperate Royalists shinning up that, either.

My historian friend was talking eloquently about the battle, but for the last few minutes I had not heard a word he said, for my own invisible antennae were picking up something in the courtyard itself which was very uncomfortable. There was a dread in the place, and it was steadily growing. I tried to withdraw my attention, to concentrate on the peace of the valley and the mellow warmth of the late summer sun; and to listen to my guide. But it was no use. The longer we stood there, the more powerful grew the feeling of anguish. In my notes that night I wrote: 'I felt something approaching pain. I must return there (to Newark), this time alone. I am afraid to do so.'

Now my companion paused, turned to me and pointed across the valley to the area under the hanging moor. 'It was there the army was finally cut to pieces,' he said. Without premeditation, I found myself contradicting him.

'Surely not,' I said. 'Surely they were massacred here, right under this cliff on which we are standing. And here, too — even worse — in this very courtyard.'

He looked at me, surprised. 'No, no, I don't think so. You are mistaken. The authorities agree that it was under the moor opposite. Why do you say there were killings in the courtyard? The executions took place later in Edinburgh.'

'Can't you feel it?' I said. 'The sense of pain and fear are intense here, almost insupportable. It's as though one could hear their cries.'

His gaze now was curious, astonished. 'You obviously feel something,' he said, 'though I'm afraid history does not agree with you.'

I said no more, beginning to wonder if I were deceiving myself, and almost immediately we left. But the sensation of misery and horror stayed with me for the rest of the day and well into the night, and although I felt foolish at having contradicted history in public, as it were, I could not shake off the sensations I had experienced in the shadow of the castle.

It was a week before I returned that way, having in the meantime, toured the handsome Lowland country from one side to the other, feeling an affinity with it which may have been an inheritance from my family's own Scottish Lowland ancestors. They, too, were of the Graham clan, as it happened. Coincidence merely.

Then I was back in Selkirk and ringing my local historian acquaintance.

'Have you found anything more to tell me?' I asked.

'Yes, indeed I have. I was hoping you'd get in touch. You remember you said the last of Montrose's army was slaughtered beneath the Newark escarpment and I said the site was on the far side?'

'Perhaps I was wrong,' I said.

'No. You were right. I have since looked up a contemporary account of the battle. The final slaughter was under the castle cliff. And what's more . . .' He paused.

'Go on. What about the courtyard? Was I wrong about that?'

'I rather wish you had been, for what I found was a bit unnerving. The camp-followers and some of the men were actually executed in the courtyard itself. Some that night and others the following morning — men, women, young boys, small children. A regular butchery. That must have been what you picked up.'

We were both silent after that, for there was nothing more to say.

I did not tell him that I intended to visit the castle again, for this time I meant to go alone, and to listen in to any further information the place might have. Human company, however pleasant, has its own vibrations, requirements, responses, and would have destroyed any hope of fulfilling this intention.

I returned to Newark on the following Sunday morning. The good people of the area would all be in church, I assumed, and I should have the castle — the New Wark or Work — to myself.

And so it proved. The late summer sun shone into Yarrow Vale, and touched the castle with smudges of cream and white; the air was warm and faintly scented. I stopped the car, got out and walked to the square keep over springy moorland vegetation, wondering as I went what the Auld Wark had been like before its replacement by the New in the early fifteenth century. The high top towers had now all but crumbled away, but enough remained of the turrets to hint at original grandeur. Newark was twice included in the dowry of Scottish Queens, first of Margaret of Denmark and second of Margaret Tudor, sister of Henry VIII of England. The Scotts of Buccleuch, though, were the hereditary keepers of Newark and the present owner is the Duke of Buccleuch. These thoughts were not in my mind, however, as I drew nearer the castle, for I was determined to try to enter the place, in spite of the fact that I knew its great door was barred, as were its lower windows, and that a number of notices warned visitors against entering on the grounds of unsafe masonry. It was not until I had almost reached the main door that I abandoned any idea of entering. There were people inside already, for I could hear the rise and fall of their voices. I paused, listening, but although the lilt and emphasis were plain, I could not quite distinguish the words. How strange! How could they have entered with barbed wire and bars as obstacles? There were several voices, but most distinctively a man's and a woman's. And presently there were just these two alone. I decided to move round the side of the tower in an attempt to glimpse the speakers. Yet as soon as I did so, the voices dissolved away. All that remained was the sound of doves and the harping of the wind. Haunted, but not this time by Montrose's unfortunates. No soundless cries now from the place the locals call Slain Man's Lea or from the once bloody, now grass-covered, courtyard. The ghosts were from some other time — earlier or later, I could not tell which.

Maybe, as Walter Scott said in his *Lay of the Last Minstrel*, Anna, Duchess of Monmouth lived here. For when Charles II's natural son by Lucy Walter, James, Duke of Monmouth, came of age, he made a Scottish alliance by marrying Anne or Anna, heiress to the Scotts of Buccleuch. Monmouth, handsome charmer though he was, was less worldly-wise than his father. He foolishly rebelled against his uncle, James II, and was subsequently executed. His widow must have known Newark Castle well, since she appears to have been born there. The idea so captured Sir Walter's imagination that he set the scene of The Last Minstrel's Lay boldly in Newark.

> He passed where Newark's stately tower
> Looks out from Yarrow's birchen bower:
> The Minstrel gazed with wishful eye—
> No humbler resting-place was nigh.
> With hesitating step at last,
> The embattled portal-arch he passed,
> Whose ponderous grate, and massy bar,
> Had oft rolled back the tide of war.

I lingered near Newark for a long time. I did not venture in. Nor did I hear the voices again, although I walked twice more around the building listening for that human sound.

To this day I have no clear idea what I encountered there. That the two experiences related to different historical periods, I am certain. And that the first at least was connected with the Philip-haugh battle I have no doubt.

Another view of Newark, where the author of this book experienced a psychic happening.

141

142

THE QUEEN'S HOUSE

Greenwich

By the early seventeenth century the Royal Palace of Greenwich was in a poor state of repair. Built by Humphrey, Duke of Gloucester, Henry IV's youngest son, it had been used continually as a royal residence, though now its two hundred years had left their mark and there seemed little to do but demolish it.

It had some claims to distinction, however, for Henry VIII had been born there, and also his daughters, Mary I and Elizabeth I. Henry, in fact, had married his first wife, Catherine of Aragon, in the palace, and his bovine fourth, Anne of Cleves.

Greenwich was a pleasant place in which to live, since it lay near to the river, and Elizabeth in particular was fond of it, spending much time here and using the Thames as a regular highway when she wished to move to Whitehall, Hampton Court, Richmond or Windsor.

The Royal Naval College now occupies the site of the old Greenwich Palace, with the elegant little Queen's House lying just beyond, and appearing to join together the two halves of the college buildings.

Originally the Queen's House was built by Inigo Jones for Henrietta Maria, Queen Consort of Charles I, and when at the end of the seventeenth century Mary II proposed to found a hospital for disabled Royal Navy servicemen, it was desired to incorporate the earlier building into the later. Sir Christopher Wren, the appointed architect, designed two handsome colonnades to link the existing palace with the Queen's House, building above each colonnade a fine dome. The view of and from the house is thereby preserved, and an elegant symmetry distinguishes the overall design.

The Royal Naval College became established in the old hospital in 1873, and there have been occasional reports of the sighting of a woman, wearing a red wig and a low-necked Elizabethan dress walking in the college's precincts. Since the figure also wears a small crown, it is thought to be that of Queen Elizabeth herself, though according to Peter Underwood, the reports are few and unsubstantiated.

Underwood is much more definite on the subject of the Queen's House haunting, for The Ghost Club, of which he is President, became involved in a detailed investigation of an incident there.

The building possesses a beautiful flight of stairs known as the Tulip Staircase, leading from ground floor to upper storey and balcony. Although parts of the building are open to the public, the Tulip Staircase is not, access being roped off at its foot.

In 1966, a clergyman, the Rev R.W. Hardy, brought his wife over to England from Canada, and in a round of sightseeing they came to

opposite
Henrietta Maria, Queen Consort to Charles I

Greenwich to view the National Maritime Museum and the delightful Queen's House.

The Hardys were much taken with the fine staircase and decided to photograph it. The stairway was, of course, empty, and was lit by the late afternoon light supplemented by an electric candelabra. However, the photograph was not developed until their return to Canada, when the couple were astonished to see what looked to be either one or two shadowy figures present upon the stairway, apparently climbing it. Quite clear on the banister rail could be seen a ringed hand.

Yet they knew beyond doubt that no living thing had been on the Tulip Staircase when the photograph had been taken.

Eventually The Ghost Club came to hear of the matter, and after negotiation with the authorities concerned, held a night-long vigil at the house, with the intention of investigating the area, and if possible replicating the Canadians' photographic results. The Club had previously submitted the Hardys' photograph to Kodak, since the film used had been one of that firm's products. The photographic experts who examined it were of the opinion that no trickery could have been involved and that the picture could only have been of persons who were actually present on the stair. Yet there had been no one on the stairs according to the Hardys.

A view of the colonnades, designed by Sir Christopher Wren.

opposite
The beautiful seventeenth-century Tulip Staircase. A ghost – perhaps that of Henrietta Maria – was once photographed climbing these stairs.

overleaf
The Queen's House, Greenwich, completed by Inigo Jones in 1635.

145

I have not personally seen a copy of this photograph, but descriptions seem somewhat confused as to the number of figures present, and not completely clear as to their positioning. What is plain is that the left hand grasping the rail wears a ring. There is thought by some observers to be a suggestion of malevolence in the positioning of the figure or figures.

Members of The Ghost Club, plus the senior museum photographer, spent their night taking photographs of the staircase in still and ciné-photography. Thermometers also were employed to detect possible falls in temperature and several doors were sealed with cotton. The staircase rail was, in addition, coated with a thin layer of petroleum jelly so that any mortal fingerprints would be recorded. These and other devices should have ensured that no psychic activities could occur in the neighbourhood of the stairs without the investigators being aware of it.

The result? Certainly no evidence definite enough to prove the haunting of the Tulip Staircase. But odd things did happen during the vigil. Several members of the group heard the distinct sound of footsteps — sounds which did not emanate from their own team. There are also reports of museum attendants who have heard similar noises over the years, though there do not appear to have been any accompanying sightings.

There has been some suggestion that the figure with the bejewelled hand may represent a monk, for it seems that the site of the Queen's House was once occupied by the house of an abbot, the manor of Greenwich being then in the possession of the Abbots of Ghent. If this were so, then one would be surprised if the staircase in a medieval abbot's house were in exactly the same physical position as the seventeenth-century Tulip Staircase. And, in fact, Underwood remarks that the staircase in the photograph does appear to be extraneous to the present one.

But before we triumphantly cry *'quod erat demonstrandum!'* it is as well to bear in mind the comment of J.A. Brooks, himself a writer on the subject of hauntings and a professional photographer of almost thirty years' experience. Brooks casts doubt on the possibility of taking such a photograph as that obtained from the position and with the timing specified by the Rev. R.W. Hardy, stating that to secure a sharp picture from so awkward a position, with an exposure of four seconds, would almost need supernatural powers on the photographer's part.

So — an unresolved haunting and an unexplained picture. Yet on several occasions photographs have been taken which revealed persons who were certainly not present at the time of the shot, the best known of the type probably being that of the Brown Lady of Raynham Hall, Norfolk. A staircase was involved here, also, a shadowy female figure appearing to be descending the steps in the photograph.

The Queen's House with the colonnades linking it to the old Greenwich Palace (now the Royal Naval College).

As for the Queen's House, if the figure(s) seen on the Tulip Staircase actually have a *psi* origin, then who is represented by it or them?

Apart from ancient monks, a suggestion was made by a medium, a friend of Peter Underwood, that a murder had once taken place on those stairs, the perpetrators of the crime being a jealous woman and an ally identified only as 'Viscount Kensington', who had planned to kill the mistress of the woman's husband.

Other suggestions are that a violent quarrel between a young couple living in the building many years ago is responsible, during the course of which their infant son was dashed from the upper floor down to the mosaic one below.

Yet a third theory is that the stair-climbing spectre may have been that of the Queen for whom the house was built, Henrietta Maria. All that is necessary for verification here is to find a portrait which shows Charles I's consort wearing the ring which appears in the controversial photograph; a ring worn on the third finger of the left hand and therefore probably a wedding ring. No such portrait is so far forthcoming.

The Queen's House, Greenwich, keeps its secret. It is, nonetheless, a delectable place to visit, and the Tulip Staircase may easily be appreciated for its own beauty and artistic worth, apart from any echoes it may still retain from the past.

RICHMOND PALACE

above and opposite:
**Gateway leading from
Old Palace Yard to
Richmond Green.**

London

Little remains of Richmond Palace now, although once it was a favourite home of Elizabeth I. Old Palace Yard can still be seen, through the gateway which faces Richmond Green. As for Richmond itself, it is a busy suburban town on the outskirts of London.

The indomitable Elizabeth died at this palace and in the process gave rise to a ghost story in her own lifetime.

After a long reign and life, Elizabeth in her sixtieth year showed little sign of conceding to age — riding, hunting and dancing almost as vigorously as ever. Perhaps such activity was a mere protest against growing old, as may have been her refusal during the winter of 1603 to wear the sensible warm garments recommended by her ladies-in-waiting. She clung obstinately to the thin

Another view of the
(restored) remains of
Richmond Palace.

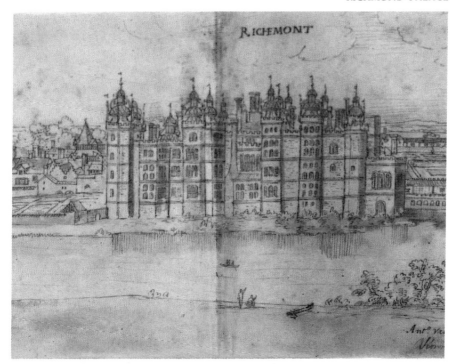

Richmond Palace (from a print in the Ashmolean Museum).

taffety and cloth of gold and silver, and not until she had caught a chill would she consent to move from the freezingly damp Whitehall Palace to the slightly milder clime of Richmond. The chill was to be her last.

When her condition worsened (pneumonia seems a likely suspect) the remarkable Queen refused to take to her bed, but sat on cushions on the floor. Then when her attendants protested, she made them haul her to her feet, and there she stood, unmoving, unspeaking, for thirteen hours, only her fierce will keeping her in position. At the end of that period she finally allowed herself to be put to bed. She did not rise from it again, but lay supine, occasionally delirious, and slowly relinquishing the bonds of her long, astonishing life.

Yet as she lay there, an extraordinary interlude occurred. A lady-in-waiting (thought to be Lady Guildford), seeing the Queen asleep or unconscious stole out to make a brief return to her own apartments. She had not even reached them before she saw the figure of her sovereign striding towards her down the corridor, the quick, light steps unmistakable. Startled, the woman looked away, perturbed and puzzled. When she turned back, there was no sign of the Queen or of any other presence than her own.

She immediately ran back towards the royal bedchamber. The Queen was exactly as she had left her and still apparently sleeping.

Now, four hundred years and a great deal of parapsychological

opposite
Queen Elizabeth I who died at Richmond Palace and whose ghost haunted the Gatehouse for a time. (Portrait by M. Gheeraerts the Younger.)

experience later, we recognize the phenomenon as astral travelling, a curious experience which can occur to individuals in times of grave illness or following severe accidents — or, occasionally, surgery — when the energy or consciousness or soul seems able to detach itself from the physical form and move and act independently of it in space. The occurrence is also known as an out-of-body experience (o.o.b.) and is well documented in the annals of all reputable psychical research societies. These experiences are comparatively common and may also occur in time of mental or emotional stress.

Elizabeth the Queen finally drifted from sleep into death. Afterwards her ghost haunted the gatehouse at Richmond for a time. It was from this place that her ring was thrown down to the rider who would take it to the son of her dead cousin, Mary, Queen of Scots, bringing him at last to the English Kingdom for which he had longed. He was James VI of Scotland and would become James I of England.

Richmond Green

THE ROYAL PAVILION

Brighton

opposite
The ornately decorated
Banqueting Room, Royal
Pavilion, said to be
haunted.

Prince George Augustus Frederick was as a young man, handsome, gallant and endowed with pleasing charm. He was also, although something of a dandy, reasonably slim and active. This truly princely figure and personality was to degenerate through over-indulgence in idleness and the sensual occupations which are often its accompaniment, until he became obese, repulsive and heavily afflicted by gout; less the 'Prinny' of public affection than the 'fat friend' of Beau Brummell's disparagement.

This particular Prince of Wales, born in 1762 son of that interminably reigning monarch, George III, was not ungifted, being musical, artistic, intelligent and cultured. He had as acute an eye for a fine painting as for a pretty woman, for a handsome building as for a well-tailored coat. That he was not always able to indulge his tastes was largely due to his acute financial difficulties, for he was perennially getting into debt, and it was not until he was given his own establishment and allowance that prospects began to improve — though, alas, only temporarily.

The Prince first bought Carlton House, near St James's Palace, London, and began to turn it into an expensively attractive home. When this project was well under way, he decided that he also needed a seaside residence, and thereupon acquired an old farm-house in Brighton, which he gradually transformed into an oriental Pavilion in which to give his out-of-town parties.

One would think any haunting of Prinny's Pavilion would carry an echo of his raucous private life. However, this seems only indirectly to be the case, since the only known haunting relates to a twentieth-century banquet which took place between the two World Wars.

The caterer in charge of this function called at the Royal Pavilion beforehand to check that all arrangements were in order. He was making some minor adjustments to a floral decoration when something prompted him to glance up from his work; whereupon he saw a dark roundish shape, apparently female, appear from the direction of the kitchens and begin slowly to tour the tables, as though checking that their layout was correct. The figure seemed to pay particularly anxious attention to the top table. After a final worried glance around, the shape disappeared through an adjacent door. The caterer, whose suspicions had been aroused by this apparently unauthorized visitor, had been following her as closely as he could get, which, no matter how he tried to narrow the distance, was never less than twenty to thirty feet. However, although he now ran to the door, opened it and peered down the long corridor beyond, he found no one in the passageway. He next

overleaf
The Royal Pavilion,
Brighton, built for the
Prince Regent, who
haunts it.

159

George IV as a young man (from the painting by Sir Thomas Lawrence), and a caricature of him (by James Gillray) in later life.

Humorous sketch by John Leech of Martha Gunn, known as 'The Brighton Bather' (first published in *Punch*). Her ghost may haunt the Royal Pavilion.

THE GOOD LITTLE BOY.

Bathing Woman. "MASTER FRANKY WOULDN'T CRY! NO! NOT HE!—HE'LL COME TO HIS MARTHA, AND BATHE LIKE A MAN!"

hurried to the entrance at its farther end and inquired of the attendant if he had seen an old lady pass him and go out. But the answer was that no one had gone by for the last hour. Mystified, the caterer returned to the banqueting room, convinced that any old lady, however spry, could have vanished without being seen by the attendant, and doubly puzzled as to why she should have been prowling through the state rooms so late at night in the first place.

Later, the caterer gave to a friend a detailed description of the woman he had seen. She had worn a long, 'bunchy' skirt, a triangular shawl and a floppy bonnet, an outfit which suggested a Regency costume, and set the two men searching through a file of old clippings and prints in the hope of finding a facsimile of the old dame of the banqueting room. Finally they discovered what they sought, and at once the caterer recognized her. 'That's her!' he exclaimed, 'Bonnet and all!' The picture was of one Martha Gunn, known as the Brighton Bather, though the reason for the title is not clear, unless, as the friends assumed, she had bathed the prince at some time in his childhood. An unlikely assumption, without further evidence, one would have thought.

My own guess is that the figure seen may have related to a former servant at the Royal Pavilion — a sometime housekeeper, perhaps, who had in life been charged with table arrangements for the Prince's vast dinner parties. After all, one small bunchy figure wearing full Regency dress is much like another. And why should Martha Gunn have had any special place in the Royal Pavilion's history?

The Prince himself is said to haunt a subterranean passage beneath his oriental-fantasy palace, though how and for what purpose is not known. There are no recent, substantiated reports of this haunting, and there seems to have been only a single sighting.

St James's Palace, London, built for Henry VIII.

ST JAMES'S PALACE

London

The site of St James's Palace was originally occupied by a convent hospital dedicated to St James the Less, and intended for the reception of some fourteen maiden lepers who were to lead a holy life, 'living chastely and honestly in divine service'. The foundation may possibly pre-date the Norman Conquest.

The land on which the Lazar House stood was green and marshy and suitably isolated from other buildings. Eventually, as leprosy began to die out in Europe (the Crusades had been partly responsible for its rapid spread) the need for specialized hospitals grew less. The land and hospital of St James came into the possession of Eton College and was held by them until 1532, when Henry VIII purchased the site in exchange for lands at Chattisham in Suffolk. The old hospital was then demolished and the leprous women removed elsewhere, an act consistent with Henry's mopping-up of the monastic order and its revenues.

On its site, Henry built himself a manor house, surrounding it with a brick-enclosed park and naming the new establishment St James's in the Fields. The initial of his second wife appears along with his own in the little which now remains of the Tudor building. The Chapel Royal contains several groups of such royal initials painted on the ceiling by Holbein for the King and completed in 1540, by which time Anne Boleyn had been dead for four years.

Time and change have affected great alterations to this palace, and now the only parts remaining of Henry's manor house are the great gateway fronting St James's, with its clock tower and twin turrets, and a few adjoining walls behind the façade. These, plus the Chapel Royal, are Henry VIII's legacy.

In Stuart times the Park if not the house, was much used by Charles II as a pleasure-park, and he would feed the waterfowl or play bowls here, sometimes accompanied by his brother, James, or by his cousin, Prince Rupert. Both the royal brothers found a use for the apartments in the palace itself, by pensioning off two of their former mistresses and setting them up in honourable retirement here.

Hortense Mancini, Duchess of Mazarin, had been one of Charles's later mistresses, 'a famous beauty and errant lady'. Madame de Beauclair had been admired and loved by James II. Now, elderly, with their years of glamour long behind them and their patrons dead or exiled, the women were thrown much into each other's company and became close friends. Inevitably, the subject of death and the hereafter came into their conversation from time to time, and a pact was made between them that whoever should die first would, if possible, return to inform the other what kind of afterlife awaited her.

The Duchess of Mazarin predeceased her friend, but in the half-hour before she died, Madame de Beauclair reminded her of their joint pact, and this the Duchess acknowledged. She would return — if she survived.

Several years passed and, with the non-appearance of her old friend, Beauclair grew bitter and cynical. There was, she told acquaintances, no survival of death, for Mazarin's promise had not been kept.

After the Duchess of Mazarin's death Madame de Beauclair had

become friendly with another influential woman (possibly the Duchess of Cleveland), and it was to this person's house that a messenger came one evening, summoning the lady to go immediately to Madame de Beauclair as she believed herself to be about to die. The lady, initially irritated and unconvinced, eventually returned with the servant to St James's Palace, only to find Beauclair seated in a chair, appearing perfectly healthy. However, the latter explained that her strong presentiment of impending death was the result of having recently seen the Duchess of Mazarin. 'I saw her stand in the same form and habit she was accustomed to appear in when living,' in one corner of the room, and the spirit had informed her that 'between the hours of 12 and 1 this night you will be with me'. There had been no time to question before the spectre vanished, leaving a deeply perturbed Madame de Beauclair behind it.

Although her visitors could see no change in her, Madame de Beauclair begged them to stay until the hour appointed, and refused to have her fears allayed. With good cause, for shortly after midnight her countenance changed, she cried out 'Oh, I am sick at heart,' and within half an hour was dead, presumably of heart-failure. The apparition's prediction had been accurate.

There is no account of any later sighting of this phantom, for it is of the typical 'message' kind. Once its information is delivered no more is heard of it.

St James's Palace does contain the echo of a later event, however, and one of a highly unpleasant nature.

Of all George III's many children, perhaps the least loved and most feared was Ernest Augustus, Duke of Cumberland, who was born on 6 June 1771, and sent abroad at fifteen to the University of Göttingen in Hanover. His career, as far as such princely careers went, was to be in the army, and he was said to be both brave and intelligent, qualities which his brothers also exhibited. However, he alone possessed an extra dimension to this family courage — a quality of attacking ferocity which perfectly suited him to his chosen profession.

In addition, he was a true die-hard Tory with no liberal feelings towards the common people, had a reputation as an extreme military martinet and was said to be as much of a womanizer as any of his disreputable brothers. In time the populace of England came to credit Cumberland with all manner of dark and hidden vices. He was without doubt the most unpopular of the royal princes.

However, the shadows in which the Duke's life had so far been conducted were presently dispersed by a blaze of publicity. On 31 May 1810, his valet Sellis was found dead in St James's Palace, ostensibly a suicide, but with the circumstances such that this theory was hardly tenable.

Rumours at once took wing. The Duke had seduced Sellis's

opposite
Ernest Augustus, Duke of Cumberland, son of George III. The ghost of his murdered valet haunts St James's Palace.

167

daughter; or the Duke had been found by Sellis in bed with the latter's wife. In the resulting scene, Sellis had (a) tried to murder the Duke and had then committed suicide, or (b) the Duke, incensed at having his liaison interrupted by a mere valet, had attacked and killed Sellis.

The facts, as far as they could be ascertained, were that on the evening of 30 May Cumberland had been attended by Sellis before leaving for a concert at 9.30 p.m. and the valet had then been dismissed for the night. At 10.30 one of the maids had seen Sellis, partially undressed, standing in the door of his bedroom, and a little later the same girl had heard someone moving stealthily through the state apartments adjoining the Duke's bedroom. Cumberland himself returned from the concert about 12.30 (according to his own account of his movements) and some time later was awakened from sleep by two blows on the head. He thought it might be a bat which had flown into him, but the receipt of two subsequent blows caused him to get up. According to his statement a light was burning in the room, but he did not see anyone. He made for the door leading to the bedroom of his second valet, Neale (named as Yeo or Yew in some accounts) and thereupon received a cut on his thigh with a sabre. The Duke called out 'Neale, I am murdered!' and the second valet thereupon dashed in to look to the Duke's wounds.

Once these had been dealt with, someone was sent to rouse Sellis, but the latter was beyond arousing, lying in his bed with his throat cut from ear to ear. According to the Sergeant of the Guard called at the inquest, 'a bloody razor' was found 'lying by Sellis's hand'. Sellis himself was dead.

Now according to this, the pro-royal account, the Duke's injuries were serious and must have been inflicted by a vicious attacker. And surely Sellis's suicide was proof of his guilt.

The popular version of events, though, favoured another view. Could any man sound asleep have survived so determined an assault with a sabre? And the flutterings of a bat? Unlikely. And why if Sellis committed suicide was his razor, the supposed instrument, actually found several yards away from his bed? The Duke's 'serious injuries', according to this version, were remarkably slight — apart from a deepish cut on one hand, which might or might not have been self-inflicted.

The two accounts of this nightmarish evening have as many discrepancies as the best of whodunits, and ultimately deciding on the likely truth is a matter of credibility. The Duke was a cavalryman and therefore a good swordsman; Sellis's head was almost severed from its body, as though by a single sabre blow. The razor was in the wrong place for a suicide's hand to have left it; the Duke's wounds were not consistent with an almost-successful murderous attack. Sellis was in any case a small, puny man, his master tall and powerful.

The inquest jury, plebeians to a man and therefore probably antipathetic to all the Duke stood for, were yet conditioned, as were all their class in that age, to 'know their place'. They were hardly likely to accuse one of the royal princes of murder. The jury did not even retire, but dutifully brought in a verdict of suicide against Sellis. A neat enough solution. In this way no one was accused of murder, actual or attempted. Only Sellis's name had been blackened and he was safely dead.

The truth will never be known, for the royal servants were, as usual, loyal servants. However, for long afterwards the Duke of Cumberland was openly booed whenever he appeared in the streets.

For many years afterwards this section of St James's Palace was said to be haunted by the ghost of Sellis, appearing as in his last earthly state, with throat cut, and with the sickly-sweet smell of blood emanating from him. There have been sounds, too, of scuffling and cursing. I know of no recent reports of these events, so after the passage of a hundred and seventy years the recording of that particular horror may have dwindled into oblivion.

Sandringham House, Norfolk. Its ghosts include a 'pulsating paper bag' and a page-boy.

SANDRINGHAM HOUSE

Norfolk

The only personal private home in England owned by Her Majesty The Queen is in the north-west of Norfolk. 'Very flat, Norfolk', the redoubtable Noel Coward once said. And so it is, in the main. But not around the Sandringham estate, for here modest hills roll beautifully to give the illusion of a Derbyshire-in-miniature. In between and around the feet of these hills fit the contours of the main Sandringham lake, and the compactness of this rural landscape plus the neatness of the many well-proportioned cottages which decorate it, suggest less a royal residence than a marvellously well-run and cared for country estate. There is something almost toylike in its immaculate quality; grass of deepest green with no blade out of place; trees trimmed and pruned to perfection; drives

170

weedless, paths swept clean, every building fully-pointed and repaired. One is afraid to breathe on it in case the whole thing, like the mythical Brigadoon, should vanish into the thin East Anglian air.

Sandringham, as you will have gathered, is neither a palace nor the property of the Crown. It is a charming smallish country house and estate belonging to a highly competent landowner who, coincidentally, also holds down the job of Monarch of Great Britain and the former Commonwealth.

By royal standards the estate has not been long in the Family, for it was only towards the end of his life that the Prince Consort purchased it, and it was first seen by his son, Albert Edward, Prince of Wales, in 1862, shortly after his father's death. It was to grow into the affections of his descendants remarkably, in spite of its initial dampness and chill and the raw winds of winter which whistled down upon it uninterrupted from Norway.

The winds and weather have changed little, but Sandringham House has been transformed since the mid-nineteenth century. It is now centrally-heated, warm, comfortable and an ideal and much-loved personal retreat for the Sovereign each New Year.

It also has its ghosts, though they are fewer in number than those belonging to the great state palaces; and, generally speaking the echoes they represent are both more domestic and happier. Occasionally at Christmas time, activities of a lively poltergeist nature have been reported, though these are always confined to the servants' quarters, and nothing seems to have been heard of them for some years. Anthony Hippisley-Coxe, in his *Haunted Britain*, also refers to a 'pulsating paper bag' or 'a grotesque lung' having been seen, but I have been unable to find any other reference to this phenomenon.

An occurrence far more interesting took place a few years ago, shortly after the present Queen had had alterations made to the original structure of the house. The old kitchens had been highly inconvenient and these were pulled down to be replaced by new. Much publicity was given to the work at the time, particularly by newspapers local to East Anglia. Nothing, however, was said about one of the curious by-products of the renovations, and I learnt of it from an eminent member of the Royal Family.

It seems that after the renovations were completed, with their consequent upheaval to the house and its inhabitants, a house party was held at Sandringham. One of the women guests was allocated a bedroom which had never produced any complaints from users prior to this time, yet this particular guest did not sleep well. She awoke one night at about 2.00 a.m., to find the room apparently illuminated. If she had been half-asleep then, the next occurrence brought her to full wakefulness. The door of the bedroom opened and a young boy came in, carrying with him what seemed to be a long pole to the end of which was attached a device which the watcher could not clearly see. The child then proceeded to walk methodically around the room, pausing every few yards to reach up to the wall with his pole, and when it was about sconce height, either to light or snuff non-existent candles. (In fact the action suggests extinguishing rather than lighting.)

I suggested to my royal informant that the child may in life have been a page, perhaps of the late eighteenth or early nineteenth centuries, whose duty had been to attend to the lights in this way, and she agreed that this was a possibility. The woman guest had not been at all afraid of her small visitor, but had watched the proceedings greatly intrigued, until the whole scene vanished and she lay in darkness once more.

It is a common occurrence for alterations to old buildings to cause the removal of a long-standing haunting; and occasionally, as in the Sandringham case, to start a haunting where none has been known before. Either way, the explanation seems to lie with the familiar 'tape-recorder' theory. Where a set of actions has been repeated regularly over a period of many years, or where some action involving strong emotion has occurred, the continual repetition on the one hand or the intensity of feeling on the other seems able to impress itself upon a part of the surroundings, which then retains that impression indefinitely, much as a tape would. If the 'recording' part of the surroundings is unhindered by obstacles, then it may be capable of radiating out in the form of energy waves the original impression of the action. And these waves in turn may be picked up by a suitably 'tuned-in' brain in the area and translated back into sound and vision to reproduce the original pattern. A television receiver has a 'scanner' built in for this purpose, and some biologists think the human brain may possess a similar mechanism.

If, however, the recording area is tampered with, say by renovations which remove or damage 'the recorder', then action which has up until then been replayed (i.e., producing a so-called haunting) will cease. Or if an obstacle which has shielded the recorder is removed, thereby enabling its emission of energy to be received, then a haunting may well begin where none existed before. I know of several cases of hauntings being destroyed by physical alterations to the surroundings, and two or three (including this at Sandringham) where the opposite is true, so that a haunting begins where none previously existed.

Occasionally there have been rumours of sightings of the ghost of Dorothy Walpole at Sandringham (she who is reputed to be the 'Brown Lady' of Raynham Hall) but these are unsubstantiated and seem unlikely.

A few of the houses on the Sandringham estate have stories of their own. One such relates to a spectral dog haunting the environs

The lake at Sandringham.

of Anmer House, home of the present Duke and Duchess of Kent. The animal is said to have been heard running, accompanied by the sound of a rattling chain; less an imprisoned dog than one which has broken loose from its chain and is bent on escaping.

Appleton House, originally known as Appleton Hall, was rebuilt by King Edward VII for his youngest daughter, Maud, wife of King Haakon of Norway, and given to the couple as a wedding gift. In the process the sixteenth century Paston gateway and dovecot were destroyed. Maybe the house's ghost was abolished in the process, for the old Appleton Hall is said at one time to have been haunted by the spectre of a woman. Nothing is known about this haunting now, and it must be presumed to have died out.

One final ghost from the royal house itself is reported by Helen Cathcart in her interesting *Sandringham*. It is said to have been seen in high summer by Prince Christopher of Greece in one of the

173

house's more modern bedrooms near the clock tower. The Prince had been resting before dinner, when in his dressing-table mirror he caught sight of the head of a young, beautiful woman, who wore a small black mask through which she gazed, her expression sad and pleading. The Prince's valet had passed by the mirror without seeing the lovely face reflected in it. Christopher's sister, Princess Marie, and the English Princess Victoria, disbelieved this ghostly tale, but presumably retracted when on visiting Houghton Hall the next day the Prince recognized the mirror-lady in the portrait of a Cholmondeley ancestress, and identified both the dress she wore and the mask she held as those he had seen in the mirror. Helen Cathcart, as it happens, is scornful of both these stories, and their credibility would certainly depend to some extent on Prince Christopher's own personality and character. *If* he saw the mirror-image, and *if* it were confirmed the next day by a portrait, what he experienced was more likely to be precognition than haunting.

Sandringham, though not a beautiful house, is a remarkably solid and comforting one. It is one of the least haunted royal homes, and when I last saw it, both house and grounds exuded serenity and security. The tenants are well-cared for by their landlords and there is a kind and warm relationship existing between them.

As I left, the royal dogs had just been let out for exercise. An assortment of labradors, retrievers and terriers raced after their keeper over the lawns and gravels. It was a pleasant, domestic and reassuring country scene.

SUDELEY CASTLE

Gloucestershire

Some two hundred years after the Romans withdrew their legions
from Britain, the Angles and Saxons moved in to the vacuum they
had left. Since the country had to be administered and the concept
of one central government was an impossibility, the land was
divided into seven 'kingdoms', though the 'Kings' were more in the
nature of tribal chieftains than the royal rulers of recent times.

One of the central kingdoms was known as Mercia and its
eighth-century king, Offa, was to find a place in history, not only as
a military leader — he had built the formidable Offa's Dyke defen-
sive work — but as an ambitious and able ruler. He also chose as
his capital, Winchcombe, in what is now Gloucestershire, and
founded a nunnery there.

175

In medieval times the nearby manor and estate of Sudeley became the property of Ethelred Unraed ('the Unready') and of his daughter and her descendants, and from that time seems to have been intermittently in royal possession, although the first Baron Sudeley was an Admiral of the English fleet in the reigns of Henry V and Henry VI. It was this man, Boteler by name, who rebuilt the first structure at Sudeley and made the fine castle whose remains are still visible today.

However, Boteler was a Lancastrian and during the supremacy of the Yorkists in the Wars of the Roses was forced to hand his handsome castle to the king, Edward IV.

Renaissance politics were a seesaw, and the defeat of the last Yorkist king, Richard III, at Bosworth was radically to alter the destiny of Sudeley. The Tudor line produced Henry VIII, whose two successive wives (Catherine of Aragon and Anne Boleyn) each gave birth to unwanted daughters, Mary and Elizabeth, thus failing to give their lord his required heir. Henry, selfish as are most pragmatists, discarded both and married one of Anne Boleyn's ladies-in-waiting, Jane Seymour, who justified his choice if not his

Ruins of the Medieval Banqueting Hall, Sudeley Castle.

opposite
Sudeley and its lake framed in a gateway.

KATHARINE PARRE

ruthlessness, by bearing him a son, Edward.

Henry's pleasure reflected fortunately on Jane's family, and her younger brother, Thomas, was made Lord Seymour of Sudeley; though this can have mattered little to Jane, for she died some twelve days after the birth of the baby, Edward.

Henry VIII would marry three times more, and his last spouse Catherine Parr, survived him. She was, in a sense, a curious choice for the lascivious Tudor monarch, having been twice widowed before she was thirty and been courted by Thomas Seymour before the King's eye fell her way. Well-educated, a linguist and a cultured woman, she seems to have been both experienced and mature, for she showed Henry's two daughters kindness, and succeeded in persuading their father to reinstate them as legitimate princesses.

After Henry's death in 1547, Tom Seymour, who had also been watching the young Princess Elizabeth with some interest, transferred his matrimonial intentions once again to her stepmother. To achieve a king's widow would be a fine step forward in the world, and he was anxious to oust his formidable elder brother, Edward Seymour, the Duke of Somerset and Lord Protector of the young King Edward VI.

The couple were secretly married at Chelsea and Catherine with her ladies-in-waiting, including the Lady Jane Grey, moved her household to Sudeley Castle. Tom Seymour himself, however, continued a surreptitious and not-quite-innocent flirtation with the Princess Elizabeth, only fifteen years old at the time.

Catherine, at thirty-five expecting a child of her new marriage, gave birth to a daughter, Mary, on 30 August 1548, but about a week later died of puerperal fever. She was given a magnificent burial in the chapel at Sudeley with Lady Jane Grey one of her chief mourners.

There she lies still, though her husband, Thomas, is buried elsewhere having fallen victim to his own ambition. After Edward VI's early death he had supported the scheme to replace the legitimate heir, the Princess Mary, daughter of Henry VIII and Catherine of Aragon, with Henry's sister's granddaughter, Lady Jane Grey. The plot had collapsed and at the instigation of the Lord Protector (Tom Seymour's elder brother, Edward), the main conspirators had been executed, including the ambitious Thomas Seymour of Sudeley.

These were the great days of Sudeley, and their echoes and reflections are still moving through the grand house which has grown from the blend of its ancient and modern history.

Much of the medieval stronghold has gone, 'slighted' by the Roundheads, as a penalty for its royalist affiliations and for sheltering Charles I during the Civil Wars. Prince Rupert, too, had used it as a base during his campaign in Gloucestershire. There would be no general regeneration until Victorian times, when the castle was

opposite
Catherine Parr who died at Sudeley Castle and whose tomb lies in the chapel there. (Portrait attributed to W. Scrots.)

restored to something of its former comfort though not to its full Tudor grandeur.

One would expect the historical echoes to belong to Queen Catherine's life here, and in a curiously unexpected way they do, though not in a parapsychological sense. True, a dignified room with Tudor accoutrements is known as Catherine Parr's nursery, but although one or two of the castle's guides suspect that some essence of the Queen remains in this area — and one said that here, if anywhere within the building she would not be surprised to encounter a ghost — the haunting associated with Sudeley is of much later date. The figure, which has been seen on several occasions, is that of a Victorian servant woman, dressed in a long grey dress, striped pinafore and mob cap, and is said to have been a housekeeper employed towards the turn of the nineteenth and during the early twentieth centuries.

At this time in its history the then owners followed the aristocratic custom of leaving their country residence for London during the season, and it was then that the servants would be under slacker discipline while they were left to clean the house in readiness for their employers' return.

It was the custom in Sudeley, as in most great houses of the time, for the women's and men's sleeping quarters to be in different parts of the building for the sake of propriety. The housekeeper at Sudeley, a highly efficient and strong-minded Scot named Janet, appointed herself in charge of the welfare of the housemaids, and it was her custom to sit at the top of the stairs leading to their quarters when the family were away, in order to fend off any approaches by the young menservants.

It seems that she still continues to do so.

The most authentic report of a psychic encounter with this personage relates to the visit of a school touring party two years ago, among whom was a girl of about twelve. The girl had climbed the flight of stairs (formerly leading to the maidservants' quarters) and had reached the landing at its head, when she saw a servant woman, complete with long dress, striped apron and mob-cap, standing in her way. This personage held a feather-duster, which she brandished in a threatening manner, twice thrusting it into the girl's face. The child, not surprisingly, became hysterical and had to be taken to lie down until she recovered from the shock.

Several members of the castle's staff corroborated the details of this incident in conversation with me, and one of the estate's former employees (now elderly and retired) said the description of the ghost fitted the former housekeeper-cum-general organizer whom he remembered simply as Janet. He had been a very young man at the time and she an elderly woman. 'She has been dead these forty years,' he said. He himself had seen her only in her real-life form, and was inclined to disbelieve in her ghostly self.

However, the figure in grey dress and striped pinafore has been seen on several occasions and most persuasively by the child with the party of tourists.

When viewing the house in company with a friend and one of the castle's senior lady guides, I experienced a series of minor shudders of the 'a goose walked over my grave' variety on passing through this particular landing. I did not know that this was the supposedly haunted area until immediately afterwards. I had a strong impression then that the schoolgirl had approached the stairhead from the opposite direction from that which tourists now use, and that the girl had therefore seen the figure differently angled from the way one might have expected. On questioning, the guide confirmed that the direction of touring the house had been reversed, and that when the child visited Sudeley, she would have come from the direction I suspected. Although I saw nothing, I had the feeling that something is still psychically active in the area of this landing.

This particular haunting appears to be of the anniversary type, occurring usually in August or September each year.

Yet this late echo apart, there seems still to be some essence lingering of the Queen who once lived at Sudeley. After Catherine Parr's death (ostensibly in childbed), the inevitable rumours circulated that she might not have died naturally. Her demise had been timed too conveniently for her husband's ambitions. To be set free of one wife when he had just formulated matrimonial designs for the next (the Princess Elizabeth) was more of a coincidence than even those rough times could tolerate. But suspecting that Queen Catherine had died of poisoning and proving the fact were different matters. She *had* borne a child, Mary, and *had* died shortly afterwards. And her widower was Lord High Admiral of England. The matter was not pursued judicially.

History had long passed over and forgotten these rumours, save in a few professionally interested circles; among which was a group of Cambridge scientists who, a few years ago, applied for and received permission to exhume the Queen's body in an attempt to determine the true cause of her death.

So it was that a small scientific team came to the castle and opened the tomb of Catherine Parr, sole survivor of Henry VIII's six wives and possible victim of a later husband.

The Queen had been embalmed after death, as was the custom for great personages, and when the lead coffin was opened her body was found to be in a perfect state of preservation. Yet the effect of air, light, moisture, at once began to take hold and the corpse visibly deteriorated, first a tooth falling out, then a lock of hair. The scientists carried out their work swiftly, and the result was startling. After tests, Catherine Parr's body was found to contain a large quantity of arsenic.

When the suggestion was made that this may have been a result of the arsenic-laden cosmetics of the time, the scientific response was that the amount of poison discovered was too great to have resulted from this cause; that something extra had almost certainly been added.

The official version is still that the Queen died at the age of thirty-five of puerperal fever following the birth of her daughter. Significantly, perhaps, the widower did not attend the funeral. The child of the marriage vanished from history, and is thought to have been disinherited and to have died in infancy.

No other verifiable ghosts haunt Sudeley, though a skeleton is said to have been found in the dungeon of the dungeon tower. This last is the same type of punishment block as that employed at Holyroodhouse. Prisoners would be taken to the top of the tower (some sixty feet high) and executed by being thrown down through an open shaft to the pit at its foot. There are no known hauntings associated with this building at Sudeley.

The only other possible haunting relates to an elderly man wearing modern dress, seen on one occasion seated outside on the castle's terrace where he stayed for an inordinately long time, unmoving. When a guide went out to ask if he needed help, she found he had disappeared, although he could not have walked out of sight in the time it took her to reach the terrace. However, this is too slight an incident to do more than arouse mild curiosity, and is not likely to constitute a genuine psychic occurrence.

Sudeley Castle is a beautiful and a peaceful place. When we visited it, a small fountain was playing in the herb garden known as The Queen's Garden; a gardener in the distance attended an enthusiastic bonfire; and near the old ruined medieval tithe barn a large ornamental pool bore shields of lilies and provided shelter for some elderly and indolent carp.

A summer place, a house of beauty and tranquillity. One of its several incongruous secrets is the fact that male heirs to Sudeley appear to die young. Out of the last eighteen heirs, thirteen have been women.

A lock of Catherine Parr's hair is still preserved within the castle. One is surprised by its fresh and Titian brightness. I had not known she was red-haired.

THE TOWER OF LONDON

If any place holds the history of Great Britain encapsulated within its walls, it is surely the Tower of London. The oldest of its buildings, the central keep known as the White Tower, was built by William the Conqueror as a fortress from which he could control the city and protect it from outside attack. This formidable structure is the only one wholly Norman, for inevitably the conglomerate of buildings now referred to as the Tower of London arose piecemeal over the centuries, as need demanded.

The Keep or White Tower is at the heart of the complex and has been variously used as royal apartments, state prison, armoury and museum; it also at one time included a torture chamber to house the rack and other implements of 'persuasion'; it still includes the Norman Chapel of St John, one of the Chapels Royal. Henry III developed much of the fortress complex which remains today, and it was he who was responsible for whitewashing the central Keep, thus giving it its present name.

At later stages in its history, other areas of the Tower fortress housed the royal menagerie and the Royal Mint, though neither were to be permanent residents. Perhaps the longest residential duty of the Tower has been to guard the royal regalia, and the

The White Tower – the central keep and oldest part of the Tower complex. Over the centuries it has housed Royal apartments, a museum, a state prison, a menagerie and a torture chamber, all of which have echoes in its hauntings.

Crown Jewels are still kept there, protected now not just by human vigilance but by the invisible eyes and ears of high technology.

To the visitor viewing the Tower of London for the first time the initial impression is of its immense age; the second impression may well be more sinister, for even without a detailed knowledge of the place's history there is an air of confinement, separateness, infinite loneliness and abandonment, which seems to emanate from the very walls.

It is therefore no surprise to a first-time visitor to learn that the

Traitors' Gate, said to be haunted by Sir Thomas à Becket

Tower is one of the worst haunted places in Britain; that it has carried with it into the present most uncomfortable echoes of its past; or that these very echoes, arising as they do, from the emotions and actions of great personages in historical times, can in turn tell us something about the way our ancestors lived, thought and behaved.

Many of the accounts of inexplicable happenings are well-known and much repeated, and I shall mention them only briefly here before examining more recent experiences of the Tower's modern inhabitants.

Among the earliest known apparitions is that of St Thomas à Becket, who is said to have appeared twice during the building of the watergate known as Traitors' Gate and the tower over it. The saint apparently disapproved of the activities and on each occasion reduced the work to rubble by striking it with his cross. However, Henry III, whose grandfather had been responsible for Becket's death, finally built an oratory into the building and named the whole work after the martyred Archbishop; whereupon the building was left undisturbed.

186

The Wakefield Tower, which stands along the stretch of walkway known as Water Lane, once held the imprisoned King Henry VI, the gentle, ineffectual Lancastrian unfortunate enough to reign during the Wars of the Roses. He was murdered by persons unknown, while praying in the small oratory attached to his rooms on the night of 21 May 1471. This murder was blamed on the Yorkist Duke of Gloucester (later Richard III), through there is no proof of his involvement.

Richard was also blamed for the deaths of his two nephews, the twelve-year-old King Edward V and his nine-year-old brother Richard, Duke of York. Richard of Gloucester had assumed the throne when the marriage of their father, Edward IV, to their mother, Elizabeth Woodville, was declared invalid. The children thus bastardized, could not by law inherit the Crown, and were therefore set aside and moved into the Tower, which was still a royal residence. For some time they were seen at the windows and battlements playing. When they ceased to appear, the rumour spread that they had been murdered, probably by smothering. And who else, it was rumoured, but their wicked uncle King Richard, would have done such a deed? Yet this is one instance where rumour was probably wrong, for there are several other candidates for the role of Little Princes' Murderer. Richard himself would have had little to gain, since he already ruled and his nephews were no threat to his power. Two children's skeletons were discovered (incomplete, being a mixture of human and animal bones) in 1674, buried under an outer stairway of the White Tower, and were thought to be those of the Princes. These remains were reinterred in Westminster Abbey.

The spirits of the little boys have occasionally been seen in the Bloody Tower, the site of their imprisonment, where, dressed in white nightgowns, they stand silently hand in hand before fading back into the stones.

One of the best known of the older hauntings is also one of the least explicable.* It occurred in 1817 in the Martin Tower to the then Keeper of the Crown Jewels, Edmund Lenthal Swifte and his family, who were seated at supper. The only illumination came from two candles on the table, and all doors and curtains were closed. Mrs Swifte had been about to drink a glass of wine when she saw a curious cylindrical object 'like a glass tube' according to her husband, containing a dense fluid coloured white and pale blue. This object continually revolved, mixing its colours as it did so. As the family gazed, petrified, the thing began to move around the table until it passed behind Mrs Swifte's chair, where it paused at her right shoulder. The woman screamed then, saying the thing had seized her shoulder, although she could not at the time see it.

* See also Clarence House, p.56.

opposite
King Henry VI, murdered in the Wakefield Tower on 21st May 1471 while saying his prayers.

above
A room in the Bloody Tower.

Throughout, only Swifte and his wife perceived the apparition, neither the wife's sister nor the couple's young son, both of whom were present, experienced anything untoward. The apparition seems to have been visible for only about three minutes before it faded and vanished.

There have been numerous incidents reported of balls and patches of mist appearing in haunted premises,* but this fluid-filled cylinder seems unique in the history of hauntings. It would seem to have represented some form of energy or consciousness, however, in view of its movement, and apparent seizure of Mrs Swifte's shoulder.

An apparition of a bear was also seen on one occasion in this same Martin Tower, a probable reminder of the days when the fortress housed the royal menagerie, precursor of the London Zoo now based in Regent's Park.

The walk on either side of the Martin Tower is known as Northumberland's Walk, since it was an exercise area for the ninth Earl of Northumberland, a fellow-prisoner of Sir Walter Raleigh. The Earl's ghost has been seen gliding along this Walk on several

opposite
The staircase in the Bloody Tower. The nephews of Richard III are thought to have been smothered in an upper room and carried down these stairs.

* See Holyroodhouse, p.114

occasions and the likelihood of its presence caused the sentries to patrol this area in pairs rather than singly.

A most persistent spirit is that of Anne Boleyn, second wife of Henry VIII, whom that unpredictable and vicious monarch discarded on her failure to give him a male heir. Although officially the charges against her were treason, adultery and incest, there is little doubt that these were merely face-savers for a King who was beginning to form a lifetime's habit of ridding himself of inconvenient wives. The Black Crow, as she was known by a populace which regarded her as a harlot and usurper, was a woman of beauty, intelligence and ambition, and Henry's match for passion and vitality. It is hardly surprising, therefore, that the violent ending to her life should have had psychic repercussions which still continue. She has been seen in the form of a headless female figure (identifiable only by its dress) drifting near the Queen's House (a building in which Anne was confined for the four days before her execution); and again heading a procession of lords and ladies as they moved down the aisle of the nearby Chapel of St Peter ad Vincula, close to the execution site itself. Anne would have known the chapel in her lifetime, for she spent the happy days before her coronation in the royal apartments of the Tower. She would, as it happened, lie after death beneath the altar of this same chapel; a consummate irony. Of all the Tower's ghosts, perhaps this one is the most persistent, elusive and disturbing, challenged, as it has been on several occasions, by sentries with fixed bayonets whose final charge at the figure has resulted in the bayonet striking only the cold stone beyond.

Yet another reputed ghost is that of the seventy-year-old Countess of Salisbury, 'the last of the Plantagenets', an elderly Catholic and innocent of any political crime, whom Henry VIII executed in revenge upon her politically active son, Cardinal Pole. The old lady, royal to the last, refused to lay her head on the block like a common traitor since she was none, and tradition has it that she ran from an inept and blundering executioner and was pursued by his hacking axe until he had hewn her to death. An unlovely picture and a gruesome end to a long life. The haunting here is given alternately as either a re-enactment of the scene itself or as the shadow of a giant axe which falls across the area. It seems likely that a reproduction of this Tudor horror may have occurred on only one occasion, though which form the haunting took there is no way of knowing.

Many who found themselves prisoners in the Tower had become so through their religion (when it differed from that of the reigning monarch) or because of their connections with the royal succession. Indeed, the succession bedevilled English history for centuries, causing both personal and communal bloodshed. The throne and its power were a prize men considered worth dying for.

But not only men died. Women in the line of succession were just

opposite
Margaret Pole, Countess of Salisbury, 'last of the Plantagenets', who was executed on Tower Green.

Some of the people who were confined in the Tower and subsequently died there: Lady Jane Grey *(above)*, Sir Walter Raleigh *(above right)*, Lord George Jeffreys (Judge Jeffreys) *(right)*, whose ghost is said to have pushed a Yeoman Warder downstairs.

The sub-crypt – former torture chamber of the Tower.

above
**Henry VIII's armour.
(Once, a Yeoman Warder
was startled by the sound
of Henry's gauntlet
tapping against its glass
case.)**

above right
**A Yeoman Warder
indicating the site of the
scaffold and block on
Tower Green where,
among others, Anne
Boleyn and Lady Jane
Grey were executed. In
the background is the
Chapel of St Peter ad
Vincula.**

as much endangered. Henry VIII's second daughter, Elizabeth, spent some time in the Tower when her elder sister Mary feared she might threaten her own right to the throne. Princess Elizabeth escaped the axe, but her cousin, Lady Jane Grey, was less fortunate.

Since Jane Grey was the granddaughter of Henry VIII's younger sister, Mary Rose, she therefore on the death of the boy Edward VI, came into the line of succession to the crown, though the next and natural heir was Henry's daughter Mary, child of Catherine of Aragon. Mary, however, was a Catholic, while Jane was strict Protestant. Moreover, the powerful and ambitious John Dudley, Duke of Northumberland, had married off his son Guildford to the fifteen year old Lady Jane, and then persuaded the dying Edward VI that she and not the Catholic Mary should be nominated as his heir. So on Edward's death it was Jane who was proclaimed Queen. But a few proclamations at church steps and market cross avail little if the majority of your countrymen prefer another candidate. The English people knew Mary Tudor and not Jane Grey to be the rightful heir and made their wishes plain by rising in her support. Jane, who was Queen for ten days, not nine as is often supposed,

194

One of the Tower ravens.

was arrested with her husband and sent to the Tower. Mary assumed the crown of England.

Lady Jane was lodged in the home of Nathaniel Partridge, Gentleman Gaoler of the Tower, next to the Queen's House. From the window of her room she watched her young husband go to his death on Tower Hill, and after a while saw the body being laid in a cart with the head wrapped in a cloth. Later she watched both return again within the Tower walls for interment in the Chapel of St Peter ad Vincula. Preparations for her own death later that afternoon were already under way on Tower Green. The date was 12 February 1554.

Guildford Dudley's wraith has, according to an old story, been seen at least once in the Beauchamp Tower, weeping quietly, as its original may have done in the hours before his death.

Lady Jane's ghost appeared as recently as 1957, on 12 February, the 403rd anniversary of her death. A certain Guardsman Johns, on duty during the early hours of that morning, heard a rattling sound somewhere above him, and looking up, saw a white shape forming itself on the battlements into the semblance of a young woman. He identified it as a likeness of Lady Jane Grey, for she had been imprisoned in a house which once occupied this site. Thinking he was hallucinating, Johns attracted the attention of another sentry,

195

who then also saw the figure.

This was a brief incident, but it may well be that some echo of this innocent victim of family ambition does remain, for one of the Yeoman Warders now living in the house which Jane Grey occupied as a prisoner told me that in 1985, on the exact anniversary of Jane's death, the main curtains in his family living-room fell to the ground. There was no reason for their sudden collapse as far as he could see, and the occurrence made both him and his wife thoroughly uneasy. He mentioned, also, that in one room of the house he and his son had each on separate occasions heard the sound of heavy breathing. The latter may have no connection with Jane Grey, of course, since she was not the only prisoner to have occupied space in this block.

I spent an entire day in the Tower of London — though not, thank goodness, a night — a warm, beautiful July day, from its opening time until almost the time of closing, and talked to many of the regular staff who inhabit and guard this strangest of royal fortresses.

Of the many men and one woman to whom I talked, only one professed absolute disbelief in the Tower's well-documented psychic life. And even he told me of an extraordinary event which had occurred to a colleague. This particular warder, whom my informant did not name, was on duty in the Byward Tower, the gatehouse which is now the Tower of London's main entrance and the fortress's guardhouse. The man happened to look up from whatever work engaged him, and was astonished to see four or five 'Beefeaters', of a much earlier period in time, seated round a log fire smoking long pipes. The whole setting appeared quite different from that of his own time. Being somewhat scared he passed a hand over his eyes, thinking to dispel the hallucination, as he supposed it; yet when he looked again the little group was still present. The man then went hurriedly out of the room, took a turn or two outside and came back some time later: to find that the scene had reverted to normal — no doubt to his relief.

Although this is a strange occurrence, it resembles a timeslip in its duration rather than a haunting, though it is not always easy to differentiate between the two.

Another Yeoman Warder also has reason to remember the Byward Tower. He was on night-watch guard there on a bleak February night in the winter of 1982/3. The time was about 2.30 a.m., and outside a heavy snowstorm was in progress with a fierce wind blowing the blizzard into drifts. So strong was the wind that earlier in the night the candle in the warder's lantern had blown out, somewhat to his consternation. 'It was', he said, 'the beginning of a strange night.'

Later, as he sat in the guardroom, the handle of the passage door (a glazed door connecting guardroom with its approaches) rattled.

This, however, he attributed to the wind. At about 2.30 a.m., something prompted him to glance at the door. He was astonished to see on the farther side of it a figure looking into the room; it was the unmistakable form and face of Sir Walter Raleigh as his portrait hanging in the Bloody Tower portrays him. The figure was in colour and solid-looking. It remained there a few seconds, to the warder's discomfiture, and then vanished.

Some eighteen months later an identical apparition was seen by another warder, and in the same place.

Raleigh, during his many years' imprisonment in the Tower, had had considerable freedom of action, and under one lenient governor had been allowed to wander at will, visiting friends and acquaintances also imprisoned in the fortress. Had the Byward Tower, one wonders, been one of his regular calling points? Perhaps for a quiet smoke or a drink with cronies or friends among the guards? Raleigh, a cultivated man with an interest in science and the arts, not only wrote his famous *History of the World* for the then young Prince of Wales, but set up a distillery through which he could prepare various potions and cordials for medicinal purposes. An active and purposeful man, Raleigh would have created something positive from the most unpromising surroundings. However, the King, James I, disliked him and on a dubious charge of treason had him beheaded on 29 October 1618. Yet Raleigh's is one of the Tower's most persistent and ubiquitous ghosts, its shadowy form appearing in the places the courtier knew in life. It has been seen on several occasions in the Bloody Tower itself, the site of his prison rooms, and on the battlements which he used for exercise.

St Thomas's Tower is not only associated with the eponymous saint, but seems to have collected an additional spectre. A deputy governor of the Tower had his quarters in St Thomas's Tower, and on one occasion when he and his wife were returning to their home after a stroll, they were stopped by a Yeoman Warder who asked if they had visitors in their quarters. On their replying in the negative, the warder said he had just observed a face looking down at him from one of the windows. Unperturbed, the Brigadier's lady merely replied. 'Oh, is it there again?' Apparently the face had been seen several times before, but never when the rightful occupants were actually in the house. A very curious circumstance, this.

I asked several of the Yeomen Warders their feelings on having to live as well as work in the Tower, and the response was that it was tolerable provided they could escape at least once a week from the premises. Having listened to some of their home-based experiences I felt the 'once a week' needed multiplication by three.

One family living in a Tower property within the walls heard sounds coming from their kitchen. On investigating, they discovered drawers of the kitchen furniture opening and shutting one

after the other, without benefit of human agency. The first time this occurred they were considerably shocked, but since the incident has been repeated several times since — always at New Year — they are becoming inured to the events. In any case, they occasionally hear from the same area the sound of a woman singing what appears to be an Elizabethan song, and they have come to think that singer and drawer-opener may be one and the same; and 'she' an earlier inhabitant of their own house.

It is this same warder who is required as part of his duties to clean the Bloody Tower. 'There is always an "aggressive" atmosphere in the upper room there,' he said. These were once Raleigh's quarters, but were later occupied by Lord George (Judge) Jeffreys of the ill-famed Bloody Assizes which disposed of the Monmouth rebels. Jeffreys had gallstones and was often in great pain. Towards the end of his life he had a barrel of brandy brought in and drank the entire contents within a fortnight, dying of its effects.

This particular warder was halfway down the turret one evening when he received a sharp push in the back which caused him to stumble and fall two or three stairs. He was convinced this was Jeffreys's doing, as in his opinion only Jeffreys would in his lifetime have been aggressive enough to take such action. Looking at that cold, remote seventeenth-century countenance, one can credit its owner with an impatience which might not stop at violence. I wondered privately how anyone had the nerve to undertake evening cleaning in any part of the Tower.

Another of the Queen's Yeomen Warders told me of events in his home, which is one of the several built into the outer walls of the Tower, and known collectively as the Casemates. It seems that from time to time both he and his wife have heard the sound of a child crying. The first time they heard the sound in the house they assumed their grandchild, who was with them at the time, was responsible. However, on checking, they found the child asleep, though the noise could still be heard. On another occasion when the crying arose the grandchild was actually not in the building, and neither the warder nor his wife could account for the weeping, though both heard it. 'It sounded', said the Yeoman Warder, 'like a small boy having a very bad time.'

There is, inevitably, a traditional explanation attached to this event. In the eighteenth century, the Royal Mint was established in the Tower and several employees lived in the building. The story goes that one of these men, having caused the pregnancy of a local girl, waited until the child was born and then shut up both mother and child in order to starve them to death. This is a story about which I have reservations, for the eighteenth century is late in time for the 'walling-up' type of activity. And the sound, whenever it is referred to by the Yeoman Warders (and I heard the story from three different sources) is always described as a *child* rather than a

opposite
Executioner's axe and block.

199

baby crying. The sounds are different and distinctive.

Sometime after my discussion with Casemates occupant No.1, I talked to a second Yeoman Warder who also told me of the sound of a child sobbing, which his family have heard in their house. They had the strong impression that the weeper was a boy.

In one room this childless couple keep a record player, the case of which is highly polished. They were astonished when they began to find a child's fingerprints upon it. When these were rubbed off they later reappeared. They have found no rational explanation for the event.

They also possess a small model of a brass cannon which the Yeoman Warder had had especially made for him during his time in the army. It is, therefore, as he pointed out 'none of your flimsy imitation stuff, but the real thing.' This model generally stood on the kitchen dresser with its wheels resting behind the narrow ridge at the back intended to prevent plates sliding forward.

On the day in question, however, the solid little model suddenly flew off the dresser and hurtled through the air, narrowly missing his wife's head. 'This', said the Yeoman Warder, 'could not possibly have been accidental.'

A strange case, indeed. To hurl small objects about — and occasionally to take aim at a target — is a childish trick. And the couple have several times heard the sound of a child crying. I asked my informant then whereabouts in the Tower he lived. I was not entirely surprised when his house turned out to be in the Casemates — next door, in fact, to Casemates occupant No.1, who also hears the sound of a weeping child in his home.

It is safe to assume that at one time — the time to which the unhappy boy belongs — these two houses were one, and that the child had the run of it. But who the weeper was and what the cause of his grief we have no means of knowing.

As for the White Tower, that dominant and inescapable centre piece of the Tower of London, so much dramatic history has been enacted there, and such deeds of violence and cruelty, that it can hardly be free of their echoes. This, the oldest building of all, is also the most formidable, and those who serve it as warders, guides or custody guards need stout nerves if they are to work and patrol there in the hours of darkness. Although all old buildings produce creaks, knockings and apparently sinister sounds which in broad daylight may be explained away, yet in the case of the White Tower there still remains an unexplained residue. Two persons, for instance, have smelled a strong perfume in the area of the Norman Chapel of St John, and although the pungency and nauseating quality of the scent suggest incense, the smell seems always strongest during the hours of darkness. So far no plausible explanation for it or its timing has been offered. Graeme Rimer in an article in *Strange Stories from the Tower of London* describes this experi-

ence, together with another which occurred to the same custody guard. This took place when he passed through the sword room *en route* for St John's Chapel. As he entered it, the guard felt an overwhelming sense of physical pressure, as though some power were trying to force him out of the room. As soon as he gained the sixteenth-century gallery, the pressure lifted. About three years after this unpleasant experience, the phenomenon was repeated — in the same place and to the same unlucky man!

Another repeated phenomenon (recounted again by Graeme Rimer) has occurred on the lowest level of the Keep. Here the dreaded dungeon and torture room are reputed to have been situated. Before a terrorist bomb exploded in the Vaults in 1974 it was part of the custody guards' duty to patrol through the cannon room by the large outer door now used as a visitors' exit. The guards would then move down the stairs, through the sub-crypt and down to the far end of the mortar room, making checks on all bolts and bars as they went. This is traditionally the setting of the old torture area. One of the guards several times had the feeling of someone walking close behind him here, and this sensation would be followed by 'a cold pressure'. Always as he began the return journey, the pressure seemed to flee away from him towards the sub-crypt. This experience had also occurred to a second guard.

The Norman Chapel of St John the Evangelist in the White Tower. Its crypt was used as a prison.

201

However, when a new floor was laid in the sub-crypt in 1968, all occurrences of this type ceased. A phenomenon which is fairly common where a 'tape-recorder' type haunting is involved.

I spoke to one of the custody guards who had had a small but odd encounter in St John's Chapel itself. He had been cleaning the place on a very warm day in 1985, when abruptly he felt an extremely cold draught of air, 'as though' he said 'someone had opened a freezer door'. Yet there was nothing present in the area to account for this sudden drop in temperature.

But one of the strangest stories relating to the White Tower, was told to me during my research for a book on time and timeslips,* and it related apparently not to its past but to its future.

On 20 April 1974 two women friends were visiting the Tower and had arrived in the armoury of the White Tower. They spent some time inspecting the weapons on display, but after a while both began to find the dungeon-like atmosphere oppressive and it was suggested they return to the open air. Halfway up the steps one, whom I shall call 'T.', turned to the other and exclaimed 'I can hear children shouting'. Her friend, 'R.', replied that all she herself could hear was the murmur of conversation from the room they had just left. At this point, T. grew agitated. 'I can hear children shouting and crying,' she said. Yet still her friend failed to hear the sounds and suggested the noise must come from the grounds of the Tower. 'No, it's closer than that. They're yelling.' Her friend began to grow irritated, and said that she had no intention of going back to the armoury to see. As the tension between the two was rising, there seemed little point in continuing the discussion. They therefore returned to the outside air in search of tea and refreshments, and the affair was forgotten.

Until a month later, when a bomb, planted in the armoury by terrorists, exploded, killing and seriously injuring a number of people, including several children.

What was it T. heard? Information from the past or from the future? I believe T.'s audio-experience was precognitive; that she heard an event which *would* occur rather than one which *had* occurred. Strange and disturbing to us though precognition may be, it is not uncommon, and it may as easily be visual as audio in form. Perhaps the future is every bit as real in our everyday lives as is the past. Both, luckily, are usually well concealed from our perceptions. The present is quite enough to cope with for most of us.

One final echo from the White Tower again concerns the armoury. One visitor to it a year or so ago asked the warder on duty about the choir which was singing there. The warder was surprised, for there was no choir. The visitor, pressing the point, asked what times it usually sang. Eventually she accepted his assurance

* *The Mask of Time* (Macdonald and Jane's).

that no choir was in the neighbourhood, but one assumes she went away a puzzled woman.

The Tower of London is a puzzling place. I, having spent the morning there, went out for a quick lunch in the shadow of Tower Bridge and returned an hour later. I re-entered the complex close by Traitors' Gate, walked beneath the arch of the Bloody Tower and started up the incline beyond. Then as the White Tower came into full view, I had an extraordinary sensation: it was as though the whole huge bulk of the Keep rose, and a feeling of utter dread, of despair and horror and loneliness came upon me. The impression was momentary only, and then was dispelled by common sense and the bright warm sunlight of July, and the noise of humanity enjoying itself. But for the seconds it lasted that feeling was real. Maybe it represents the actual truth of the Tower of London.

The Chapel of St Peter ad Vincula. A ghostly procession was once seen here. (Both the Chapels in the Tower are said to be haunted.)

Aerial view of the castle
from the north-west
showing the Great Park,
the domain of Herne the
Hunter who hanged
himself from a great oak
in one of the forest rides.

WINDSOR CASTLE

Berkshire

At least one member of the present Royal Family does not believe Windsor Castle to be haunted, though she concedes that the Great Park probably is. The evidence, so far as the castle is concerned, is against her, for there have in the past been numerous reports of different hauntings connected with the building. However, to say that a place *was* haunted is not to be sure that it still is, for it is of the nature of energy-fields to fade in the course of time, and many so-called 'hauntings' appear to be fields of energy. It is certain that most ghosts and their activities seem to dwindle over the years and eventually cease to be, though a few are extremely long-lasting and persistent.

One of the latter has been seen from time to time over the centuries in the royal library of the castle. The most detailed account we have of this phenomenon comes from an experience in 1897 by one of the Officers of the then Guard. The young man's name was Carr Glynn, and he was apparently a booklover, for he visited the library for reading rather than curiosity purposes. Presently his attention was attracted by the sound of high heels clicking across bare boards. The sound at first came from a distance, but gradually grew nearer, and the young man noticed that they seemed unhesitating and purposeful, as though the owner were familiar with the route she took. Then, from the opposite end of the room, he saw the tall figure of a woman, dressed in black with a matching drape of lace covering her hair. She passed close to him, and he found himself reminded of portraits of Queen Elizabeth which he had seen. Yet at that moment Lieutenant Glynn does not appear to have thought the woman other than flesh and blood. He was, in any case, intrigued by her behaviour. She walked across to a corner of the room, turned right, then disappeared from view and he assumed she had entered an inner room of which he was unaware. Later he questioned a library attendant — perhaps feeling concern lest the woman find herself stranded in a locked library — but the man assured him that no room existed where the lady in black vanished, neither was there, as Glynn supposed, a door in that corner leading to another room. Peter Underwood, a comprehensive researcher, states that there had in Elizabeth's own day been a flight of steps leading from this corner of the library to the terrace beneath, one which the Queen herself must have used many times. It has long since disappeared, and Lieutenant Glynn was the astonished witness of an old habit of one of history's most remarkable women. And presumably of the woman herself! A double privilege.

Queen Victoria's eldest daughter, 'Vicky', otherwise the Empress Frederick of Prussia, is said to have seen this phantom, and there are stories that 'she' has also been seen by one of our present royal princesses, though since there are neither details nor confirmation available of the last rumour, it must be treated with reserve.

Another library-haunting ghost is that of George III, who, as an old, sick man, spent most of his time at Windsor. He is said to be heard muttering in a way characteristic of him in life, the thrice-repeated question 'What? What? What?' This monarch was also seen shortly after his death by the patrol of Guards whose salute he normally returned, even when at his most deranged. While his body still lay in state, this same patrol passed the King's window, and on looking up, its commander saw the unmistakable figure of George III standing there. Automatically, he gave the command 'Eyes right!' and as the heads swung round, the figure gave its customary response. A clear case, this, of immediate post-death appearance, when the surviving consciousness appears to be still attached to its old habitat, not yet adjusted to its new terms and conditions of being. This is a single appearance ghost, and when compared with the regular haunters cannot be classed in the same category.

Corridor leading to State
Apartments, Windsor
Castle.

Elliott O'Donnell, a prolific writer on ghosts, reported an account of a haunting in the castle's precincts which took place in April 1906. In the early hours of one morning a Coldstream Guard sentry saw a number of men descend the steps of the East Terrace. Suspecting them to be intruders, he issued the usual challenge, but the figures continued to walk towards him, unheeding. When the third challenge brought no response he fired at the leading figure, which paused, but showed no sign of injury. The sentry, no doubt then beyond caring about consequences, prepared to charge; when all the figures abruptly vanished. The bewildered Guardsman reported the experience to his superiors and a search was made of the grounds, without result. Whereupon the wretched, ghost-seeing sentry was given three days C.B. as punishment.

There is a long and detailed account in existence of appearances by the elderly Sir George Villiers, father of that Duke of Buckingham who was friend and favourite of Charles I. The Duke, a haughty and power-greedy man, was bitterly unpopular in the country and there were many gloomy predictions about his future.

206

George III who is said to haunt Windsor Castle Library.

Two views of the Long Walk, East Terrace, Windsor Castle. The spectre of a young guardsman is said to patrol here. Do the statues move in the moonlight?

It was on a February night in 1628 that the spirit of old Sir George Villiers appeared in the bedroom of an officer of the King's Wardrobe in Windsor Castle. The ghost instructed the man to go to his son and warn him of his danger unless he mended his ways. When the officer ignored the instruction, the apparition reappeared on the two succeeding nights, each time seeming more threatening. Finally the officer did as bidden and conveyed the message to the erring Duke: who, in the event, though disturbed, took no steps to improve his conduct and was finally assassinated by a disgruntled subaltern at Portsmouth on 23 August of that year. A warning ghost, this, appearing only to deliver a message, and when that was done, not being heard of or seen again.

The Long Walk at Windsor seems to possess the eerie quality of certain prehistoric stone circles, where the number of stones changes each time they are counted. At Windsor, the elusive units are not stones but statues, and sentries on duty in this area have several times had the impression that the things have moved in the moonlight, and that it was, in any case, impossible to count them. Moonlight, as every child and every poet knows, has the power to create illusion.

Perhaps this is why a young sentry of the Grenadier Guards grew more and more depressed by his patrol duties in this part of the

castle. He was eighteen, new to the army, and possibly feeling lonely and homesick in the grand and mysterious surroundings to which he found himself posted.

The year was 1927, halfway between the two World Wars, and an uneasy time for all Europeans. Maybe the boy was too much alone, or had no taste for army life. Whatever the reason, one night while on sentry duty on the Long Walk, he shot himself.

Some weeks later, one of his colleagues was allotted the Long Walk as his patrol area, and the man, Sergeant Leake, undertook his task in bright moonlight, probably with no thought of the recent past in mind. Towards the end of an uneventful patrol, he heard in the distance the relieving sentry marching to meet him. However, as he turned back towards his box, he saw coming straight towards him another guardsman; and recognized in the features under the bearskin cap the face of the young suicide. Then the relief patrol came into view and the dead man vanished. When Leake returned to the guardhouse, he checked his experience with the sentry whom he, in turn, had relieved from duty: only to find that the man, also, had encountered the same ghostly colleague that night. Dennis Bardens, writing interestingly of an interview with ex-Sergeant Leake reports him as saying that at the time of this experience he felt his hair 'stand on end'; as it did again when he related it so long afterwards.

The ghost of the guardsman was still actively remembered at Windsor years later when Hitler's doodlebugs chugged over the great castle, and the broken drone of enemy planes made sleep impossible for anyone between the ages of nine and ninety. A friend of mine Mr Walter ('Wally') Wyles, at that time a smart young lieutenant of an anti-aircraft battery, was stationed at Windsor Castle during the last days of the Second World War, and reluctant to be there, since the unit considered these duties were not the type of activity with which they should be engaged. They had envisaged themselves at the very least as 'fighting on the beaches' as per the Churchillian injunction, and here they were tamely guarding a royal residence. They felt slightly more endangered, however, when stationed along the notorious Long Walk, with its moving statuary and its ghostly sentry legend. Those who actually trod that haunted stretch declared the ground was wearing away at a greater rate than it should on account of the ghost's activities. Yet as far as Lieutenant Wyles knew, no one ever saw the spectral guardsman, or made any mistake about the number of marble statues.

The ghost of a long-dead policeman is also said to haunt part of the castle precincts. He has been seen many times in one particular area, where his living self apparently died of a heart attack in the early 1940s. Underwood has a detailed account of an encounter with this figure, where the percipient, a guardsman at the time, actually held a conversation with the apparition before it disappeared. (Conversations with ghosts, though rare, are by no means unknown.)

Among the minor hauntings are that by Charles I, said to have been seen near the Canon's House, and Henry VIII, whose identity has been deduced by the heavy groans and weary dragging footsteps accompanying it. (Henry's ulcerated leg gave him great pain in his latter years.)

But undoubtedly the castle's major haunting is that by Herne the Hunter, whose appearances often coincide with the onset of national disaster of one sort or another.

Traditionally, Herne was a huntsman to Richard II, and while in pursuit of a stag in Windsor Forest, saved the King from a goring at the near-expense of his own life. Yet as he lay dying, a stranger emerged from the forest and offered to heal him by magical means. The King agreed, and the wizard bound a pair of stag's antlers to the wounded man's head, undertaking as he did so, to nurse Herne back to health. The grateful King promised Herne that on his recovery he should be made head huntsman.

There are few successes which don't arouse jealousy somewhere. This time it was the rest of the huntsmen who were infuriated; to such an extent that they threatened the magician with death if he allowed Herne to live. The stranger compromised, stating that though Herne would indeed become head huntsman, he would not hold the position long. At the same time he assured the plotters that in wishing ill on Herne his curse would also follow them. They paid little attention to the threat.

Eventually Herne returned to duty, but his old skills had gone, and he had so little luck in finding sport for his master that he was dismissed from his new post. Whereupon he hanged himself from a great oak in one of the forest rides. In succeeding centuries the tree was known as Herne's Oak, and Herne himself occasionally appeared there, clad in hunting garb and wearing the stag's spread of antlers bound to his head.

Tradition has it that on stormy nights Herne and a band of ghostly huntsmen (the envious men on whom his curse fell), plus a pack of spectral hounds, can be heard in full cry through the Park and forest of Windsor. It is said, also, that from time to time the facsimile of his corpse has been seen swinging from Herne's Oak. Until the latter was cut down inadvertently in the nineteenth century, that is; since when occasionally the shadowy form of the tree, too, has appeared. A member of the present Royal Family told the author that Herne has also been seen in this century, and the Wild Hunt, which his activities represent, was seemingly experienced in 1936 by two Eton schoolboys, who, though hearing the hunt galloping towards them with full hound chorus, could yet see nothing. They did feel a draught of ice-cold air as rushing forms seemed to sweep past them. That at least was the account they gave and not all schoolboys are practical jokers.

Yet whatever Herne's hunting and legend suggest, the origins of the Wild Hunt are far, far older than the fourteenth century. For Herne is the embodiment of the Norse god, Odin or Woden, or of the horned god of the Celts, Cernunnos. The Wild Hunt itself is the mythical explanation for the great winter storms which have swept over Europe from the north for as long as man remembers. The howl of wind and the beat of rain and blizzard are the cries of baying hounds and the pounding of horses' hooves. Primitive man needed human explanations for the natural phenomena which threatened him. Best to deify Nature's uncontrollable forces and propitiate them. Who else should lead the sky hunt but the sky god, Odin? The Herne story, when it came, was terrifying enough to need similar rationalization; thus Wild Hunt and its Huntsman, Herne and his hauntings became one. And Odin, who once hung for nine days and nights upon an ash tree, became Herne, hanged by his own hand upon a Windsor oak. The common folk, consciously remembering the story of Herne the Hunter, subconsciously remembered their ancient religion and its Father God, Odin.

After the careless destruction of Herne's Oak, Queen Victoria ordered the planting of a replacement, and the legend is still current that whenever the country is in dire trouble the mysterious Herne will again make his appearance; though one cannot imagine that this will help any national crisis. He is said to have appeared before the abdication of King Edward VIII.

The Herne story is one of the examples of myth blending with parapsychology, though most accounts of ghosts and hauntings have far younger roots and arise from human behaviour, historical incident and, almost certainly, from the energy patterns set up by intense emotion.

That such patterns exist, there is little doubt, for the human energy field can be measured and even photographed, projecting as it does, to form a continuous envelope around the body at a distance of a few centimetres from its surface. This field, I believe, is one of the primary means of communication between sentient beings — older even than language — and both gives out and receives information in a two-way process. Since royal personages are as human as their subjects, the process applies to them, also, and they are therefore able not only to convey information about themselves via this field but to receive it concerning others.

If the energy field becomes highly activated under the pressure of intense emotion (hate, fear, horror, elation, love), it seems likely that the information conveyed by its 'broadcasting' may register on local surroundings and be capable of being replayed at intervals, for a greater or lesser period of time, such broadcasting to be received by any suitable subject in the neighbourhood, and its waves translated back into terms of either visual images and/or sounds.

And venerable royal homes, so frequently the scenes of conflict and tragedy in the past, most certainly hold energy records strong and numerous enough to match those of any video library.

CONCLUSION

It is difficult to define what is meant by the term hauntings. In the Introduction to this book I have referred to them obliquely as part of a hidden reality, the bulk of an iceberg whose tip is the conscious human life we live on earth. That life consists of material objects and perceptions — house, car, furniture, food, environment, place of work and artefacts connected with whatever job we do. It also consists of an awareness of other living forms which share the planet with us, beginning with our fellow-humans and progressing through animal life to the smallest insect and plant. All these are clear to our senses; we can see, hear, touch, taste, smell them, and recognize their reality by these means.

Yet what of the many experiences we encounter which cannot be classified as material? Falling in love, feeling antipathy (hatred, at its worst), knowing hope, anticipation, exultation, the wide range of emotions aroused in us by mere daily living? For want of a better definition we class them as abstracts, as we also do heroism, self-sacrifice, altruism; and cruelty, anger, sadism. These are, it is true, partly states of mind which lead to states of behaving, which in turn come to be states of being. They are not material, but they are as much a part of life's reality as the material world we frequently term the only 'real' one.

Therefore, reality appears to exist on at least two levels, even to our muffled perceptions. In fact, it exists on many more; and it is probably to these planes that the various forms of psychic phenomena belong.

Before we can consider how such phenomena operate — and hauntings seem to be among the simpler examples of them — we need to look at why they exist at all. What is *psi*? How is it produced, and in what reality are *its* roots as opposed to our own?

In this last question, perhaps we have the answer. *Psi* does not exist apart from us, is not something which operates independently of humanity; does not even operate outside the rules of physics which appear to govern all life and all known creation. I believe that all experiences and occurrences met with by humanity — and one can only speak with certainty of mankind, for this is the one form of life we know from the inside, from actually living it — arise from the nature of the atom of which all creation appears to be constructed.

In an earlier book, *The Mask of Time*, I wrote:

The world in which we live is only apparent to us because information about every single component of it is continually being sent out into space. Thus each object, each part of an object, in fact all matter, is radiating out 'waves' of one sort of another. The type of waves which enable us to see the world around us or to perceive objects in space are light waves, and they, in common with radio waves, ultra-violet rays, infra-red rays, X-rays, gamma and heat, etc., are part of a group called electromagnetic waves. All members of this group travel at the speed of light — the immense rate of 186,000 miles per second.

These 'waves' and the force called electromagnetism are not matter in the sense that they can be seen with the naked eye (our usual criterion for recognizing material objects), but they are apparently associated with it, a product of matter and radiating from it. The earth, sun, stars, a ship, and the sailor who mans her, a sheep and the grass it eats, an armchair and the cat curled in it, are all giving out and receiving energy — and, in the process, exchanging information. Energy and matter are actually two aspects of the same thing — the atomic structure of the universe itself. In this context, the mysterious 'waves' appear to represent energy.

This being so, then everything is inter-related, since all are constructed of the same material. Therefore when we ask, in what reality are the roots of *psi* as opposed to our own? The answer is that they are the same. And *psi*, whatever it is and however it operates, is as much a part of us as we of it; and all matter and energy is interconnected by this curious kinship of having had, somewhere, a common origin, the evidence for which is its shared atomic nature. So when the bored shepherd of the ballad sang 'There *must* be something more,' he was uttering a deep, though unrecognized (by him), truth.

Therefore if we start from the point at which everything in the universe is radiating information and receiving it in similar form, then we presuppose a world in which this is going on ceaselessly, day and night — communications being 'broadcast' and 'received' endlessly, because of the cosmic structure, and of the nature of life, which is a part of it.

This being so, is it then possible for some radiated communications to be retained in the environment in which they take place? The biologist, Lyall Watson, suggested in *Supernature* that we might eventually be able to build machines which recapture events of the past, just as film and recordings reproduce events of the present. But we may already have such a machine, the human brain; for it is a highly complex and balanced instrument, sending out electrical impulses of its own and receiving others from outside which it is able to translate into patterns, sometimes in terms of vision or sound, sometimes of thought and ideas; though it seems that incoming signals need to be at the right frequency — possibly matching the brain's own wavelength at the moment — before an intelligible result can be obtained. It has been suggested by one scientist that the brain may possess a scanning mechanism similar to that used in television, whereby the impulses it receives from outside may be translated to produce a visual image or sound which the receiving individual 'sees' or 'hears'.

Perhaps certain types of haunting operate in this way. If the original emotion in life produced sufficient intensity to record on some part of the adjacent environment (stone appears to be a good, long-term recording material) then presumably any human brain in the neighbourhood which happened to be functioning on the same frequency as the recorder transmitting the past events, should, in theory, be able to pick up the transmission and translate it into terms of either sound or vision or both; and would thus experience those events in their initial form: this, merely by translating the impulses into their original audio/visual patterns. This would certainly be a visitation from the past, though scarcely supernatural. The whole process would seem to be inadvertent and involuntary and not subject to any control of will.

The fact that one cannot see ghosts to order has always been one of science's complaints. Scientific methods rely on reproduction of results whenever required in order to validate theories. There may be a time when enough is understood of the mechanism of triggering and receiving a haunting, to be able to do just that. But for the present the haunting process looks to be random and refuses to conform to present-day scientific requirements.

The type of broadcast haunting I have been describing, and its probable method, relates only to the recorded type of event or emotion. Pattern hauntings — the footsteps and doors, the regular events whose sequence when experienced is always the same — come into this category. Monks or nuns processing at regular times for prayer; invisible choirs singing at what were originally precisely timed services; the sights and sounds of battles whose violent emotions have gone deep into their battlefields: all these will replay time after time with no variation and be seen and heard sometimes through several centuries, with their details always identically repeated. But not all hauntings are so predictable.

By contrast to the last, there is a second group which seems to function on the basis of freewill; that is, the ghost or ghosts do not appear to be subject to routine or precise timing, do not repeat activities *ad nauseam* in an identical pattern on each occasion, and are not (as the pattern haunters appear to be) always unaware of the living persons to whom they appear. On this count alone, they seem both more real and more alarming than the phantoms of the first group. It is this type of haunter which, very occasionally, holds a conversation with the haunted; this type, too, which often appears in such a realistic form that witnesses may not realize that what they have seen is not solid flesh and blood.* Until it vanishes, that is.

* See Blickling Hall, pp.42-3.

Although Group 2 hauntings appear to be in a minority, they contain a number of curious and uncomfortable — from the percipient's viewpoint — sub-types. If there are malevolent ghosts, then this is the group in which you will find them. And that there are such ill-intentioned hauntings is borne out by a number of cases within my personal experience, one of the worst of which concerned a fine house in Hampshire, built by a tyrannical Victorian who had determined that his family should live in it forever. The family, however, had other ideas, and on his death sold the place. After that the paterfamilias came back to haunt in a most uncivilized fashion, causing considerable detriment to the life, health and general well-being of the various people who lived in his former house over the next century. This is an extreme example, however, and such cases are fortunately rare.

Another Group 2 sub-type is the messenger ghost. Into this category come those who appear (often more than once) immediately after their deaths, sometimes to family or friends, sometimes just in the places to which they belonged in life. Occasionally, an individual of this type will turn up with the apparently express purpose of announcing his death or of saying farewell to loved ones. And when this occurs, it can be because the death has taken place a distance away, and there has been no opportunity for farewells. Often, indeed, the recipient of the information was not even aware that his visitant was not in the best of health.

Occasionally a sub-type of this kind will act as a messenger, bringing a warning of some sort. Of this kind was the ghost of the Duchess of Mazarin,* who visited St James's Palace years after her own death in order to carry out her promise to Madame de Beauclair. 'Between the hours of twelve and one this night, you will be with me,' the ghost had said. And so it proved. Ghostly prophecies are usually to be relied on; which suggests the spectres who make them have access to records of the future — as indeed we do ourselves occasionally.

Two more sub-types are (1) those which appear not to know that they are dead or, knowing, not wishing to believe it, and (2) those whose emotional attachment to a locality is so great that they seem incapable of breaking it even after death. (In a sense the Victorian tyrant came into this category.)

To make statements like those in the last paragraph, is to hint that some ghosts may actually represent the survival of human consciousness after death. I believe such a survival — at least in part and at least for a time (though it may be wholly and permanently) is almost certain. Many of the freewill ghosts seem to bear out this supposition, for they act and speak with intelligence, often give us information we would not otherwise have had and generally behave as though they were still very much alive somewhere in

* See St James's Palace, p.167.

addition to the earth-place they happen to be visiting.

As for the type whose attachment to earthly sites makes them unwilling to leave after death, one suspects that in life they may have been emotionally immature persons, reluctant to accept change and feeling safe only in familiar surroundings. Some good research needs to be done on this theory. The transition from being a creature of matter and energy (the incarnate state) to that of pure energy (the likely post-death state) must be traumatic even when one is prepared for it. Still more so when the idea of death has been both feared and strongly resisted. Or when the death has come violently or unexpectedly.

Any parapsychologist who lectures on his subject will find himself bombarded by questions afterwards. One of the commonest, if your theme has been hauntings, is that relating to ghostly intentions. Can ghosts harm the living? Can we in any way be damaged by them? My answer to this question until comparatively recently has always been that no *physical* harm is likely to result or be inflicted, but that one may suffer from fear if one does not understand what is going on. Or that if one tries deliberate meddling (again without comprehending what is involved) then there may be a boomerang effect. I am aware that this is a tricky area of investigation, but in view of the prevailing professional silence on the subject, coupled with continued public curiosity, perhaps it is time to examine the situation. I will say in advance that the following are my personal beliefs, crystallized through many years of active experience, and of reading, interviewing and writing on the subject of so-called paranormality. That these views may not be universally shared, I am well aware. They may, however, be of some value to persons still in the early stages of inquiry.

Dangers to amateur investigators and others

1. There is some risk involved in all attempts to 'get in touch' with the dead, or otherwise to conjure up something or somebody. This can involve mere disappointment at the efforts of self-deceived or even fraudulent mediums, who may in turn deceive credulous inquirers. Where the recently bereaved or grief-stricken are concerned this can be emotionally damaging, creating hope where perhaps none is justified and leading to false ideas about the whole vast and remarkable subject of parapsychology.

Many so-called séances intending to 'raise the dead' may result in the raising instead of other, unknown energy forms; or even produce a corporate (and largely uncontrollable) energy from the group of investigators themselves. It is now accepted that living individuals can contribute involuntarily to events; the poltergeist effect is an example in point, where the modern view is that the considerable energy involved in moving objects through space (technically known as psychokinesis or P.K.) and seen at its most powerful in cases of poltergeistry, may arise from the energy of living persons. In the majority of cases of this type there is likely to be an association with an adolescent child. It is this individual who appears (usually involuntarily) to 'throw off' energy charges into his/her surroundings, often with highly destructive results. One has to bear in mind here, that the time of life when human energy is probably at its most intense and least disciplined is during adolescence.

There are other circumstances in which the energy of living humans may also contribute to apparently parapsychological events. This was clearly demonstrated by the creation of 'Philip', a so-called surviving entity, which a Toronto group of inquirers in the seventies actually invented and which then began to move tables around as a proof of 'its' existence. The energy required appeared actually to come from the researchers themselves, though there was a point where 'Philip' showed disturbing signs of rebellion, exhibiting a will of 'his' own in 'his' activities. *Motto*: remember Frankenstein.

These strictures also apply to the entertainment, party-game kind of activities, ouija, planchette etc. The ouija-type séance using tumblers and letters of the alphabet can have quite terrifying results, though whether the violent energy involved in the moving tumbler comes from the inquirers themselves or some outside agency, one can never be sure — at least not sure enough to banish the strong reservations one has about it. Energy of *some* sort is present, that is certain. And no unknown energy form should be treated in so cavalier a fashion as to play foolish games with it. *Motto*: remember the Barnwell Castle case in the present book.*

2. Is there a risk involved in living in haunted houses? If badly haunted — that is, so severely as to leave an atmosphere of malevolence or horror in the area concerned — then the answer is probably yes.

To discover how this can be one has to return to the theory of energy-involvement. If hauntings are old records of intense emotion, resulting in (possibly though not certainly) an electromagnetic field in the area which can discharge itself in terms of 'waves'; and if these waves continually bombard the receptor systems of living humans, then certain effects may result. It is known that the presence of electricity pylons within a hundred yards of dwelling-houses can affect by their radiation the health of persons living in those houses. Villagers in south-west England some years ago were in this situation and constantly complained of headaches, malaise and neurasthenic symptoms. Radiation from radioactive materials had even worse effects. Even before natural phenomena such as thunderstorms or prior to earthquakes some animals and humans

* See Barnwell Castle, pp.29-32.

suffer effects which range from nausea and headache to extreme depression or agitation.

If ghosts and haunted areas are therefore radiating some form of energy (and thereby broadcasting information) then who is to say what kind of physical effect this may have on living creatures within range? And if the 'broadcasting' be constant and its original source were violent, terrifying or otherwise psychologically or emotionally unhealthy, may it not reproduce some of the effects which the original source had on those within its then orbit? This is speculation at present, for as far as I know no fieldwork has yet been done into this aspect of parapsychology.

Most serious investigators have encountered cases where long-time dwellers in badly haunted houses appear to have experienced disturbing physical and mental symptoms, sometimes accompanied by a series of inexplicable accidents and misfortunes. These may, of course, be coincidental. On the other hand if the radiation from electricity pylons can produce ill-health, and if states of physical debility can cause people to become depressed and accident-prone, who is to say where speculation ends and fact begins?

I am not saying that hauntings and the haunters themselves can cause illness, but that *if* they are energy fields, then the radiation from those fields may well affect matter within its range.

In the course of my researches for this book, two sites above all struck me as being abnormally impregnated by the fearful emotions generated in them in earlier days. They were the Tower of London (especially the White Tower) and Holyroodhouse (chiefly the James IV tower — i.e., that associated with Mary, Queen of Scots). In each case, I found the atmosphere strongly repellent, that of the White Tower conveying a sensation of despair and fear which were almost overwhelming. There was in it something destructive, partaking of total inhumanity and infinite threat.

The Holyrood feeling was differently orientated but almost more acute, and, as far as I could tell, centred entirely on the Queen's Suite, with its focal point in the supper room. And the area of that room most affected was that immediately to the left of the entrance, where the sensation of horror seemed intolerable. I was only able to bear being in that room for a few minutes at a time. The very experienced warden who was my guide, admitted that he, also, hated to stay in the room and always got out of it as fast as possible. The 'horror' patch was almost measurable and seemed to cover a circular area about a yard in diameter. Although the rest of the small room felt unpleasant enough, the heart of the disturbance appeared to be the spot near the door. Was this where Mary had sat or stood when Rizzio had fallen at her feet and begged for aid? We cannot now know. All the present writer can say is that the effect on anyone lingering within the ambience is likely to be unpleasant.

The Outer Moat of the Tower of London was filled up late in the seventeenth century. The large moat constructed by Edward I to surround the Tower (presumably the Inner Moat) was filled by order of the Duke of Wellington in 1843, as it had become a health hazard.

There are more subtle threats to human well-being than those caused by stagnant water. It would be no surprise to me if at some time in the distant future the White Tower and the James IV tower of Holyroodhouse, being condemned as hazards to public health, were quietly razed to the ground.

QUESTIONS OF RESEARCH

If parapsychology is ever to achieve parity with the older sciences, both in terms of acceptability and funding, then the scope of its research must be drastically widened. Many countries now have flourishing official centres of psychical or parapsychological research, and in Britain at last a Chair in the subject has been established. This, funded by a bequest from the late Arthur Koestler, is at Edinburgh University, with its first occupant Dr Robert Morris.

However, considering the immensity of the subject with which we are dealing (and one suspects that it may be rooted in nothing less than the atomic structure and behaviour of the universe itself), then the field of research so far would seem to have been surprisingly narrow. Some good, concentrated work on reincarnation has taken place (notably by Dr Ian Stevenson of the USA); research into dreams was long conducted by the Maimonides Dream Centre, of New York; the Toronto groups have undertaken investigations into psychokinesis; the Institute of Psychophysical Research in Oxford has done good work on dreams, general ESP and out-of-body experiences; and just about everyone professionally concerned with the subject has researched precognition. Indeed, one cannot help feeling that the enthusiasm for playing guessing games either with a machine or with another researcher some distance away has overreached itself. By this time it is surely accepted that an idea or its visual form may be propounded in one place and divined by a person separated from it by distance and physical barriers; yet the tests continue to be repeated, long beyond the point which would have seemed necessary for scientific proof and acceptance.

In the meantime, there are other areas of research, seemingly of equal importance, which have barely been touched. I would suggest the following undertakings for immediate detailed fieldwork:

1. That attempts be made to measure the human electromagnetic field or aura and to identify its wavelength in (a) its possessor's normal state of consciousness and (b) while experiencing a psychical occurrence of the haunting type. Recognized that there are difficulties attached to this proposal, by reason of the random element in hauntings.

2. That this measuring process be also applied to an area reputed to be strongly haunted, concentrating, if possible, on the epicentre of the emanation, the *exact* area where the sensation is strongest. This, again, is likely to be a time-consuming process because of the phenomena's element of unpredictability.

3. An attempt to establish the nature of the apparent inter-relationship between apparition, presence or sound in a reputedly haunted area and the recipient who appears to respond to it or them. A relevant question is, how does the activated haunting alter the electrical or electromagnetic state of (a) the core-area of the haunting, (b) the personal field of the recipient, (c) the immediate space between the two, and (d) the electromagnetic component of the room area itself? (Screening from extraneous energy influences would be necessary here.)

4. Tests to establish that the energy concerned is electromagnetic.

I should like to suggest that a recognized proportion of all researchers (say fifty per cent) involved in fieldwork, should possess a certain qualification — i.e., that they should have had at least some subjective experience of the *psi* phenomenon — preferably in the field they intend to investigate. At present, too many researchers seem never to have experienced any form of involuntary, unsought psychic phenomenon. And since there may be a difference in process between experiencing *in the course of* professional experimentation and experiencing inadvertently, in my view researchers qualified in both categories should be included in any fieldwork undertaken. To use exclusively those persons who have never undergone an unsought psychic experience is the equivalent of asking someone to round up sheep when he does not know how sheep behave. (Curious how sheep and their minders seem to have infiltrated this book.)

Some of the events chronicled here, including those related to the author by the persons who experienced them, are also subject to possible alternative explanations than those of parapsychology. However, as an experiencer myself, I can testify to the difference in the way inner or auto-communication (a self-induced or 'imaginative' event) occurs and that in which the occurrence is imposed from without. The processes are distinct, separate, recognizable, and appear not only to come from different sources, but to 'feel' differently — i.e., the channel for the information in each case is recognizably not the same.

Hauntings, though the most obvious, numerous and possibly least complex of all psychic phenomena, may turn out to be only the fringe of an enormous field of knowledge, still untapped and in twilight. As such they should neither be dismissed lightly nor treated flippantly.

BIBLIOGRAPHY

Abbott, Geoffrey:	*Ghosts of the Tower of London*	(David and Charles, 1986).
Alexander, Marc:	*Haunted Castles*	(Muller, 1974).
	Phantom Britain	(Muller, 1975).
Alice, Princess, Duchess of Gloucester:	*Memoirs of Princess Alice*	(Collins, 1983).
Bardens, Dennis:	*Ghosts and Hauntings*	(Zeus Press, 1965).
Battiscombe, Georgina:	*The Spencers of Althorp*	(Constable, 1984).
Barnett, Corelli:	*Marlborough*	(Eyre Methuen, 1974).
Blair, Peter Hunter:	*Northumbria in the Days of Bede*	(Gollancz, 1976).
Bold, Alan:	*Holyroodhouse*	(Pitkin Pictorials, 1980).
Borg, Alan. (Ed.):	*Strange Stories from the Tower of London*	(British Heritage Supplement).
Brooks, J.E.:	*Ghosts of London*	(Jarrolds, 1982).
Buchan, John:	*Montrose*	(Hodder, 1928).
Brown, R. Allan:	*English Castles*	(Batsford, 1954).
Bryant, Arthur:	*Makers of the Realm*	(Collins 1965).
Cathcart, Helen:	*Sandringham*	(W.H. Allen, 1964).
Dames, Michael:	*The Avebury Cycle*	(Thames and Hudson, 1977).
Dane, Clemence:	*Will Shakespeare*	(Heinemann, 1921).
Day, James Wentworth:	*Here are ghosts and witches*	(Batsford, 1953).
Elborn, Geoffrey:	*Princess Alexander*	(Sheldon Press, 1982).
Forman, Joan:	*Haunted East Anglia*	(Hale, 1974).
	The Haunted South	(Hale, 1978).
	The Mask of Time	(Macdonald and Jane's, 1978).
Frazer, J.G.:	*The Golden Bough*	(Papermac, 1967).
Fulford, Roger:	*Royal Dukes*	(Pan Books, 1933).
Goodman, Jean (with Sir Ian Moncrieff):	*Royal Scotland*	(Debrett/Webb and Bower, 1983).
Green, Celia, and McCreery, Chas.:	*Apparitions*	(Hamish Hamilton, 1975).
Grimbal, Pierre (Ed.):	*Larousse World Mythology*	(Hamlyn, 1965).
Hackett, Francis:	*Henry the Eighth*	(Cape, 1929).
Harvey, John:	*The Plantagenets*	(Batsford, 1948).
Hedley, Olwen:	*Prisoners in the Tower*	(Pitkin Pictorials, 1972).
	Royal Palaces	(Pitkin Pictorials, 1982)
Herm, Gerhard:	*The Celts*	(Wiedenfeld, 1975).
Hippisley-Coxe, A.D.:	*Haunted Britain*	(Hutchinson, 1973).
Hogg, Gary:	*A Guide to English Country Houses*	(Country Life, 1964).
Hole, Christina:	*Haunted England*	(Batsford, 1940).
Hopkins, R. Thurston:	*Cavalcade of Ghosts*	(World's Work, 1956).
	Ghosts over England	(Meridian Books, 1953).
Innes-Smith, Robert:	*Glamis Castle*	(Pilgrim Press, 1983).
Jenkins, Elizabeth:	*The Princes in the Tower*	(Hamish Hamilton, 1978).
Jordan, W.K.:	*Edward VI: The Threshold of Power*	(Allen and Unwin, 1970).

Kendal, Paul Murray: *Richard III* (Sphere. 1972).
Mackenzie, Andrew: *Apparitions and Ghosts* (Arthur Barker, 1971).
Marie-Louise, Princess: *My Memories of Six Reigns* (Evans Bros 1956).
Marshall, Dorothy: *Eighteenth-Century England* (Longman, 1962).
Marwick, Arthur (Ed.): *Illustrated Dictionary of British History* (Thames and Hudson, 1980).
Mattingley, Garrett: *Catherine of Aragon* (Cape, 1942).
Metcalfe, Leon: *Discovering Ghosts* (Shire Publications, 1972).
Nash, Roy: *Buckingham Palace* (Macdonald, 1980).
Norman, Diana: *Stately Ghosts of England* (Muller, 1963).
O'Donnell, Elliott: *Scottish Ghost Stories* (Jarrolds, 1981).
Palmer, Alan: *Life and Times of George IV* (Weidenfeld, 1972).
Petry, Michael J.: *Herne the Hunter* (Wm. Smith, Reading).
Prebble, John: *The Lion in the North* (Secker and Warburg, 1971).
Ross, Charles: *The Wars of the Roses* (Thames & Hudson, 1976).
Scott, Carolyn: *Westminster Abbey* (Sheldon Press, 1976).
Scott, Walter: *Border Ballads* (Routledge).
Sergeant, Philip W.: *Historic British Ghosts* (Hutchinson, 1936).
Selley, W.T.: *England in the Eighteenth Century* (A. and C. Black, 1934).
Sheppard, Edgar: *St James's Palace, Vols. 1 and 2* (Longmans, 1894).
Steadman, G. and Anker, Ray: *Ghosts of the Isle of Wight* (I.W. Country Press, 1977).
Steinberg and Evans: *Steinberg's Dictionary of British History* (Edw. Arnold, 1970).
Stenhouse, Lawrence: *Scotland's Heritage* (Collins, 1970).
Stirton, John: *Glamis, a Parish History* (W. Shepherd, Forfar, 1913).
Thompson, Francis: *Ghosts, Spirits and Spectres of Scotland* (Impulse Publications, 1973).
Underwood, Peter: *Haunted London* (Harrap, 1973).
This Haunted Isle (Harrap, 1984).
Van der Zee, Henri and Barbara: *William and Mary* (MacMillan, 1973).
Waldman, Milton: *Elizabeth and Leicester* (Collins, 1946).
Watson, Lyall: *Supernature* (Hodder, 1973).
Wedgwood, C.V.: *Montrose* (Collins, 1952).
White, R.J.: *The Age of George III* (Heinemann, 1968).
Woodward, G.W.O.: *Mary, Queen of Scots* (Pitkin Pictorials, 1973).

Also numerous brochures, leaflets, information lists, diagrams and maps relating to various properties and their histories: also extracts on Newark Castle from *The Border Magazine* of 1909.

Additional Publications

Tales from Scottish Lairds (Jarrolds, 1981).
King Arthur, Tintagel Castle (Ronald Youlton).
Prisoners in the Tower: Elizabeth Jenkins (Hamish Hamilton, 1978).
Official Guide to Oundle (Brit. Publ. Co., Gloucester, 1973).
The Spiritualist Gazette, May 1984.
The Daily Mail, 30 October 1984.
Daily Star, 8 January 1981.
Daily Express, 28 January 1984.
Daily Express, 27 January 1984.
The Spiritualist Gazette, July 1984.

By the same author

Plays
Portrait of the Late
Midwinter Journey
The Accusers
Ding-Dong-Belle
Night of the Fox
The Wise Ones
The Pilgrim Women
Three Plays for Girls
The Walled Garden
A Search for Comets

Educational Books
See for Yourself (Books 1 and 2) (History)
Galaxy Anthologies (Books 1 to 4) (Poetry)
Look Through a Diamond (Poetry anthology, Canada)
The Romans (History)

Drama (Educational, Canada)
The Freedom of the House
The End of a Dream
Westward to Canaan
The Turning Tide

Juvenile Fiction
The Princess in the Tower

General Adult
Haunted East Anglia
The Haunted South
The Mask of Time